WORKING PAPERS

Volume I, Chapters 1-10

for use with

FUNDAMENTAL ACCOUNTING PRINCIPLES

Eighth Canadian Edition

Kermit D. Larson
University of Texas-Austin

Morton Nelson
Wilfrid Laurier University

Michael Zin
Professor Emeritus
University of Windsor

Raymond Carroll
Dalhousie University

Represented in Canada by:

 **McGraw-Hill Ryerson**

IRWIN

Toronto • Chicago • Bogotá • Boston • Buenos Aires
Caracas • London • Madrid • Mexico City • Sydney

McGraw-Hill
Ryerson Limited

A Subsidiary of The McGraw·Hill Companies

©Richard D. Irwin, a Times Mirror Higher Education Group, Inc. company, 1972, 1976, 1980, 1984, 1987, 1990, 1993, and 1996

Printed in Canada by Tri-Graphic Printing (Ottawa) Limited

ISBN 0-256-17533-0

4 5 6 7 8 9 0 TRI 3 2 1 0 9 8

Contents

EXERCISE 1–2

(a)

(b)

(c)

(d)

EXERCISE 1–12

Parts 1 and 2

ASSETS						=	LIABILITIES		+	OWNER'S EQUITY	
CASH	+ ACCOUNTS RECEIVABLE	+ OFFICE SUPPLIES	+ OFFICE EQUIPMENT	+ BUILDING		=	ACCOUNTS PAYABLE	+ NOTES PAYABLE	+	CAPITAL	EXPLANATION OF CHANGE

Part 3

_____
_____
_____
_____
_____
_____
_____
_____
_____
_____
_____

Part 4

_____
_____
_____
_____
_____
_____
_____
_____
_____
_____
_____
_____
_____
_____
_____

Part 5

_____
_____
_____
_____
_____
_____

Part 2

Part 3

Part 4

DATE	CASH	+ ACCOUNTS RECEIVABLE	+ OFFICE SUPPLIES	+ PROFESSIONAL +	OFFICE EQUIPMENT	= ACCOUNTS PAYABLE	+ CAPITAL	EXPLANATION OF CHANGE

ASSETS = LIABILITIES + OWNER'S EQUITY

Part 3

Part 4

Part 5

TRANSACTION	BALANCE SHEET			INCOME STMT.	STATEMENT OF CHANGES IN FINANCIAL POSITION		
	TOTAL ASSETS	TOTAL LIAB.	EQUITY	NET INCOME	OPERATING	FINANCING	INVESTING
1.							
2.							
3.							
4.							
5.							
6.							
7.							
8.							
9.							
10.							

PROBLEM 1–7

PROBLEM 1–8

Parts 1 and 2

	ASSETS					=	LIABILITIES		+	OWNER'S EQUITY	
	CASH	ACCOUNTS RECEIVABLE +	OFFICE SUPPLIES +	OFFICE EQUIPMENT +	BUILDING +	=	ACCOUNTS PAYABLE +	NOTES PAYABLE +		CAPITAL	EXPLANATION OF CHANGE

	ASSETS					=	LIABILITIES		+	OWNER'S EQUITY	
CASH	ACCOUNTS RECEIVABLE	OFFICE SUPPLIES	OFFICE EQUIPMENT	BUILDING		ACCOUNTS PAYABLE	NOTES PAYABLE		CAPITAL	EXPLANATION OF CHANGE	

Part 2

Part 3

Part 4

Part 1

Part 2

Part 3

Name _____

	TRANSACTION	BALANCE SHEET			INCOME STMT.	STATEMENT OF CHANGES IN FINANCIAL POSITION		
		TOTAL ASSETS	TOTAL LIAB.	EQUITY	NET INCOME	OPERATING	FINANCING	INVESTING
1.								
2.								
3.								
4.								
5.								
6.								
7.								
8.								
9.								
10.								

PROBLEM 1-15

PROBLEM 1-16

	ACCOUNT	TYPE OF ACCOUNT	INCREASE	DECREASE	NORMAL BALANCE
a.	Accounts payable				
b.	Accounts receivable				
c.	B. Baxter, capital				
d.	B. Baxter withdrawals				
e.	Cash				
f.	Equipment				
g.	Fees earned				
h.	Land				
i.	Postage expense				
j.	Prepaid insurance				
k.	Rent expense				
l.	Unearned revenue				

EXERCISE 2–2

_____
_____
_____
_____
_____
_____
_____
_____
_____
_____
_____
_____
_____
_____
_____
_____
_____
_____
_____
_____
_____
_____
_____
_____
_____

Cash		Accounts Payable

R. J. Wainwright, Capital

Accounts Receivable		Services Revenue

| Office Supplies | | |

Office Equipment		Utilities Expense

EXERCISE 2–4

EXERCISE 2–5

ERROR	DIFFERENCE BETWEEN DEBIT AND CREDIT COLUMNS	COLUMN WITH THE LARGER TOTAL
(a)		
(b)		
(c)		
(d)		
(e)		
(f)		
(g)		

EXERCISE 2–7

EXERCISE 2–8 Part 1

Part 2

Part 3

EXERCISE 2-9

EXERCISE 2-10

GENERAL JOURNAL

Page 1

DATE	ACCOUNT TITLES AND EXPLANATION	P.R.	DEBIT	CREDIT

GENERAL JOURNAL

DATE	ACCOUNT TITLES AND EXPLANATION	P.R.	DEBIT	CREDIT

EXERCISE 2–12

Cash

Equipment

Wayne Oldham, Capital

Prepaid Rent

Fees Earned

Boat

Gas and Oil Expense

EXERCISE 2–13

GENERAL JOURNAL   Page 1

DATE	ACCOUNT TITLES AND EXPLANATION	P.R.	DEBIT	CREDIT

Name _____

GENERAL JOURNAL

DATE	ACCOUNT TITLES AND EXPLANATION	P.R.	DEBIT	CREDIT

EXERCISE 2-15

Cash

Land

Accounts Payable

Long-Term Notes Payable

Accounts Receivable

Avery Wilson, Capital

Prepaid Insurance

Avery Wilson, Withdrawals

Office Equipment

Fees Earned

Computer Equipment

Wages Expense

Building

Computer Rental Expense

Advertising Expense   Repairs Expense

Part 3

Name _____

Cash

Land

Accounts Payable

Notes Payable

Accounts Receivable

Wayne Seale, Capital

Prepaid Insurance

Wayne Seale, Withdrawals

Office Equipment

Excavating Revenue

Machinery

Machinery Repairs Expense

Building

Wages Expense

Machinery Rentals Expense

Land

GENERAL LEDGER

Cash   Account No. 101

DATE	EXPLANATION	P.R.	DEBIT	CREDIT	BALANCE
Mar 1		J1	25 000		25 000
1				1 800	23 200
5			500		23 700
11				3 600	20 100
15				1 500	18 600
20			1 600		20 200
27				1 800	18 400
31				175	18 225

Accounts Receivable   Account No. 106

DATE	EXPLANATION	P.R.	DEBIT	CREDIT	BALANCE
Mar 9			2 000		2 000
20				1 600	400
23			660		1 060

Office Supplies   Account No. 124

DATE	EXPLANATION	P.R.	DEBIT	CREDIT	BALANCE
Mar 3			600		600
30			200		900

Prepaid Insurance   Account No. 128

DATE	EXPLANATION	P.R.	DEBIT	CREDIT	BALANCE
Mar 15			1 500		1 500

Prepaid Rent   Account No. 131

DATE	EXPLANATION	P.R.	DEBIT	CREDIT	BALANCE
1			1900		1900

Medical Equipment   Account No. 167

DATE	EXPLANATION	P.R.	DEBIT	CREDIT	BALANCE
Mar 1			6000		6000
3			3000		9000

Accounts Payable   Account No. 201

DATE	EXPLANATION	P.R.	DEBIT	CREDIT	BALANCE
Mar 3				3600	3600
11			3600		-0-
30				200	200

Carrie Ford, Capital   Account No. 301

DATE	EXPLANATION	P.R.	DEBIT	CREDIT	BALANCE
Mar 1				31000	31000

Carrie Ford, Withdrawals   Account No. 302

DATE	EXPLANATION	P.R.	DEBIT	CREDIT	BALANCE
Mar 21			1800		1800

Accounting Fees Earned   Account No. 401

DATE	EXPLANATION	P.R.	DEBIT	CREDIT	BALANCE
Mars				500	500
9				2000	2500
23				660	3160

Utilities Expense   Account No. 690

DATE	EXPLANATION	P.R.	DEBIT	CREDIT	BALANCE
Mar 31			175		175

Part 4

Trial Balance

	DEBIT	CREDIT
Cash	18225	
Accounts Receivable	1060	
Office Supplies	800	
Prepaid Insurance	1500	
Prepaid Rent	1900	
Medical Equipment	9000	
Accounts Payable		1200
Carrie Ford, Capital		31000
" ", withdrawls	1200	
Accounting Fees Earned		3160
Utilities Expense	175	
	34360	34360

GENERAL JOURNAL

Page 1

DATE	ACCOUNT TITLES AND EXPLANATION	P.R.	DEBIT	CREDIT
N 1 1999 Cash	Owners			

DATE	ACCOUNT TITLES AND EXPLANATION	P.R.	DEBIT	CREDIT

	Utilities Expense					Account No. 690
DATE	EXPLANATION	P.R.	DEBIT	CREDIT	BALANCE	

Part 3

Part 4

Part 5

Cash

Accounts Payable

Notes Payable

Accounts Receivable

Carol Blake, Capital

Office Supplies

Carol Blake, Withdrawals

Office Equipment

Commissions Earned

Automobile

Appraisal Fees Earned

Land

Office Salaries Expense

Building

Advertising Expense

Name _____

GENERAL JOURNAL

DATE	ACCOUNT TITLES AND EXPLANATION	P.R.	DEBIT	CREDIT

DATE	ACCOUNT TITLES AND EXPLANATION	P.R.	DEBIT	CREDIT

GENERAL LEDGER

Cash   Account No. 111

DATE	EXPLANATION	P.R.	DEBIT	CREDIT	BALANCE

Accounts Receivable   Account No. 117

DATE	EXPLANATION	P.R.	DEBIT	CREDIT	BALANCE

Office Supplies   Account No. 131

DATE	EXPLANATION	P.R.	DEBIT	CREDIT	BALANCE

Prepaid Insurance   Account No. 133

DATE	EXPLANATION	P.R.	DEBIT	CREDIT	BALANCE

Prepaid Rent

Account No. 134

DATE	EXPLANATION	P.R.	DEBIT	CREDIT	BALANCE

Office Equipment

Account No. 156

DATE	EXPLANATION	P.R.	DEBIT	CREDIT	BALANCE

Accounts Payable

Account No. 211

DATE	EXPLANATION	P.R.	DEBIT	CREDIT	BALANCE

Adam Uppe, Capital

Account No. 311

DATE	EXPLANATION	P.R.	DEBIT	CREDIT	BALANCE

Adam Uppe, Withdrawals

Account No. 316

DATE	EXPLANATION	P.R.	DEBIT	CREDIT	BALANCE

Accounting Fees Earned   Account No. 412

DATE	EXPLANATION	P.R.	DEBIT	CREDIT	BALANCE

Utilities Expense   Account No. 651

DATE	EXPLANATION	P.R.	DEBIT	CREDIT	BALANCE

DATE	ACCOUNT TITLES AND EXPLANATION	P.R.	DEBIT	CREDIT

SERIAL PROBLEM
Emerald Computer Services (Continued)

GENERAL LEDGER

	Cash					Account No. 101
DATE	EXPLANATION	P.R.	DEBIT	CREDIT	BALANCE	

Fundamental Accounting Principles, Vol. I, 8th Can. Ed.

Name _____

GENERAL JOURNAL

Page 1

DATE	ACCOUNT TITLES AND EXPLANATION	P.R.	DEBIT	CREDIT

EXERCISE 3–2

GENERAL JOURNAL

Page 1

DATE	ACCOUNT TITLES AND EXPLANATION	P.R.	DEBIT	CREDIT

EXERCISE 3–3

_____
_____
_____
_____
_____
_____
_____
_____
_____
_____
_____
_____

CHAPTER 3   EXERCISE 3–5

GENERAL JOURNAL   Page 1

DATE	ACCOUNT TITLES AND EXPLANATION	P.R.	DEBIT	CREDIT

Name _____

GENERAL JOURNAL

Page 1

DATE	ACCOUNT TITLES AND EXPLANATION	P.R.	DEBIT	CREDIT

EXERCISE 3–8

GENERAL JOURNAL   Page 1

DATE	ACCOUNT TITLES AND EXPLANATION	P.R.	DEBIT	CREDIT

EXERCISE 3–11

GENERAL JOURNAL

DATE	ACCOUNT TITLES AND EXPLANATION	P.R.	DEBIT	CREDIT

GENERAL JOURNAL

Page 1

DATE	ACCOUNT TITLES AND EXPLANATION	P.R.	DEBIT	CREDIT

Name _____

Parts 1 and 2

Name _____

Cash

Accounts Payable

Long-Term Notes Payable

Accounts Receivable

Bobbie Benson, Capital

Office Supplies

Bobbie Benson, Withdrawals

Automobiles

Fees Earned

Office Equipment

Salaries Expense

Building

Utilities Expense

Land

Name _____

Part 3

GENERAL JOURNAL   Page 1

DATE	ACCOUNT TITLES AND EXPLANATION	P.R.	DEBIT	CREDIT

GENERAL JOURNAL

Cash   Account No. 111

DATE	EXPLANATION	P.R.	DEBIT	CREDIT	BALANCE

Accounts Receivable   Account No. 112

DATE	EXPLANATION	P.R.	DEBIT	CREDIT	BALANCE

Prepaid Insurance   Account No. 113

DATE	EXPLANATION	P.R.	DEBIT	CREDIT	BALANCE

Office Supplies   Account No. 114

DATE	EXPLANATION	P.R.	DEBIT	CREDIT	BALANCE

Investment in Trail, Inc., Common Shares   Account No. 121

DATE	EXPLANATION	P.R.	DEBIT	CREDIT	BALANCE

Office Equipment   Account No. 131

DATE	EXPLANATION	P.R.	DEBIT	CREDIT	BALANCE

Accumulated Amortization, Office Equipment — Account No. 132

DATE	EXPLANATION	P.R.	DEBIT	CREDIT	BALANCE

Trucks — Account No. 133

DATE	EXPLANATION	P.R.	DEBIT	CREDIT	BALANCE

Accumulated Amortization, Trucks — Account No. 134

DATE	EXPLANATION	P.R.	DEBIT	CREDIT	BALANCE

Building — Account No. 135

DATE	EXPLANATION	P.R.	DEBIT	CREDIT	BALANCE

Accumulated Amortization, Building — Account No. 136

DATE	EXPLANATION	P.R.	DEBIT	CREDIT	BALANCE

Land — Account No. 137

DATE	EXPLANATION	P.R.	DEBIT	CREDIT	BALANCE

Franchise   Account No. 141

DATE	EXPLANATION	P.R.	DEBIT	CREDIT	BALANCE

Unearned Storage Fees   Account No. 212

DATE	EXPLANATION	P.R.	DEBIT	CREDIT	BALANCE

Salaries and Wages Payable   Account No. 213

DATE	EXPLANATION	P.R.	DEBIT	CREDIT	BALANCE

Long-Term Notes Payable   Account No. 231

DATE	EXPLANATION	P.R.	DEBIT	CREDIT	BALANCE

Dennis Mead, Capital   Account No. 311

DATE	EXPLANATION	P.R.	DEBIT	CREDIT	BALANCE

Dennis Mead, Withdrawals   Account No. 312

DATE	EXPLANATION	P.R.	DEBIT	CREDIT	BALANCE

Revenue from Moving Services   Account No. 411

DATE	EXPLANATION	P.R.	DEBIT	CREDIT	BALANCE

Storage Fees Earned   Account No. 412

DATE	EXPLANATION	P.R.	DEBIT	CREDIT	BALANCE

Office Salaries Expense   Account No. 511

DATE	EXPLANATION	P.R.	DEBIT	CREDIT	BALANCE

Drivers' and Helpers' Wages Expense   Account No. 512

DATE	EXPLANATION	P.R.	DEBIT	CREDIT	BALANCE

Gas, Oil, and Repairs Expense   Account No. 513

DATE	EXPLANATION	P.R.	DEBIT	CREDIT	BALANCE

Insurance Expense   Account No. 514

DATE	EXPLANATION	P.R.	DEBIT	CREDIT	BALANCE

	Office Supplies Expense					Account No. 515
DATE	EXPLANATION	P.R.	DEBIT	CREDIT	BALANCE	

	Amortization Expense, Office Equipment					Account No. 516
DATE	EXPLANATION	P.R.	DEBIT	CREDIT	BALANCE	

	Amortization Expense, Trucks					Account No. 517
DATE	EXPLANATION	P.R.	DEBIT	CREDIT	BALANCE	

	Depreciation Expense, Building					Account No. 518
DATE	EXPLANATION	P.R.	DEBIT	CREDIT	BALANCE	

	Interest Expense					Account No. 519
DATE	EXPLANATION	P.R.	DEBIT	CREDIT	BALANCE	

Fundamental Accounting Principles, Vol. I, 8th Can. Ed.

Name _____

Part 2

GENERAL JOURNAL

DATE	ACCOUNT TITLES AND EXPLANATION	P.R.	DEBIT	CREDIT

GENERAL JOURNAL

DATE	ACCOUNT TITLES AND EXPLANATION	P.R.	DEBIT	CREDIT

Part 3

Fundamental Accounting Principles, Vol. I, 8th Can. Ed.

GENERAL JOURNAL

DATE	ACCOUNT TITLES AND EXPLANATION	P.R.	DEBIT	CREDIT

GENERAL JOURNAL

DATE	ACCOUNT TITLES AND EXPLANATION	P.R.	DEBIT	CREDIT

DATE	ACCOUNT TITLES AND EXPLANATION	P.R.	DEBIT	CREDIT

GENERAL LEDGER

Cash   Account No. 101

DATE	EXPLANATION	P.R.	DEBIT	CREDIT	BALANCE
1996 Nov. 30	Balance				22 0 3 0 00

Accounts Receivable   Account No. 106

DATE	EXPLANATION	P.R.	DEBIT	CREDIT	BALANCE
1996 Nov. 30	Balance				6 3 0 0 00

Computer Supplies   Account No. 126

DATE	EXPLANATION	P.R.	DEBIT	CREDIT	BALANCE
1996 Nov. 30	Balance				1 5 2 0 00

Prepaid Insurance   Account No. 128

DATE	EXPLANATION	P.R.	DEBIT	CREDIT	BALANCE
1996 Nov. 30	Balance				1 4 4 0 00

	Prepaid Rent					Account No. 131

DATE	EXPLANATION	P.R.	DEBIT	CREDIT	BALANCE
1996 Nov. 30	Balance				3 0 0 0 00

	Office Equipment					Account No. 163

DATE	EXPLANATION	P.R.	DEBIT	CREDIT	BALANCE
1996 Nov. 30	Balance				6 0 0 0 00

	Accumulated Amortization, Office Equipment					Account No. 164

DATE	EXPLANATION	P.R.	DEBIT	CREDIT	BALANCE

	Computer Equipment					Account No. 167

DATE	EXPLANATION	P.R.	DEBIT	CREDIT	BALANCE
1996 Nov. 30	Balance				12 0 0 0 00

	Accumulated Amortization, Computer Equipment					Account No. 168

DATE	EXPLANATION	P.R.	DEBIT	CREDIT	BALANCE

	Accounts Payable					Account No. 201

DATE	EXPLANATION	P.R.	DEBIT	CREDIT	BALANCE
1996 Nov. 30	Balance				- 0 -

Wages Payable   Account No. 210

DATE	EXPLANATION	P.R.	DEBIT	CREDIT	BALANCE

Unearned Computer Fees   Account No. 233

DATE	EXPLANATION	P.R.	DEBIT	CREDIT	BALANCE

Tracy Green, Capital   Account No. 301

DATE	EXPLANATION	P.R.	DEBIT	CREDIT	BALANCE
1996 Nov. 30	Balance				48 0 0 0 00

Tracy Green, Withdrawals   Account No. 302

DATE	EXPLANATION	P.R.	DEBIT	CREDIT	BALANCE
1996 Nov. 30	Balance				4 1 5 0 00

Computer Services Revenue   Account No. 403

DATE	EXPLANATION	P.R.	DEBIT	CREDIT	BALANCE
1996 Nov. 30	Balance				13 6 5 0 00

Amortization Expense, Office Equipment   Account No. 612

DATE	EXPLANATION	P.R.	DEBIT	CREDIT	BALANCE

SERIAL PROBLEM
Emerald Computer Services (Continued)

Amortizaiton Expense, Computer Equipment — Account No. 613

DATE	EXPLANATION	P.R.	DEBIT	CREDIT	BALANCE

Wages Expense — Account No. 623

DATE	EXPLANATION	P.R.	DEBIT	CREDIT	BALANCE
1996 Nov. 30	Balance				2 6 2 5 00

Insurance Expense — Account No. 637

DATE	EXPLANATION	P.R.	DEBIT	CREDIT	BALANCE

Rent Expense — Account No. 640

DATE	EXPLANATION	P.R.	DEBIT	CREDIT	BALANCE

Computer Supplies Expense — Account No. 652

DATE	EXPLANATION	P.R.	DEBIT	CREDIT	BALANCE

Advertising Expense — Account No. 655

DATE	EXPLANATION	P.R.	DEBIT	CREDIT	BALANCE
1996 Nov. 30	Balance				1 2 4 0 00

| | Mileage Expense | | | Account No. 676 | |
DATE	EXPLANATION	P.R.	DEBIT	CREDIT	BALANCE
1996 Nov. 30	Balance				3 7 5 00

| | Miscellaneous Expenses | | | Account No. 677 | |
DATE	EXPLANATION	P.R.	DEBIT	CREDIT	BALANCE
1996 Nov. 30	Balance				5 0 0 00

| | Repairs Expense, Computer | | | Account No. 684 | |
DATE	EXPLANATION	P.R.	DEBIT	CREDIT	BALANCE
1996 Nov. 30	Balance				4 7 0 00

EMERALD COMPUTER SERVICES

Adjusted Trial Balance

December 31, 1996

EMERALD COMPUTER SERVICES

Income Statement

For three months ended December 31, 1996

Part 6

EMERALD COMPUTER SERVICES

Statement of Changes in Owner's Equity

For three months ended December 31, 1996

SERIAL PROBLEM
Emerald Computer Services (Continued)

Part 7

EMERALD COMPUTER SERVICES
Adjusted Trial Balance
December 31, 1996

EXERCISE 4–2

GENERAL JOURNAL

Page 1

DATE	ACCOUNT TITLES AND EXPLANATION	P.R.	DEBIT	CREDIT

FINE PAINTING CO.
Work Sheet
For Year Ended December 31, 1996

ACCOUNT TITLES	UNADJUSTED TRIAL BALANCE		ADJUSTMENTS		ADJUSTED TRIAL BALANCE		INCOME STATEMENT		STATEMENT OF CHANGES IN OWNER'S EQUITY AND BALANCE SHEET	
	DR	CR	DR	CR	DR	CR	DR	CR	DR	CR

GENERAL JOURNAL

DATE	ACCOUNT TITLES AND EXPLANATION	P.R.	DEBIT	CREDIT

ACCOUNT TITLES	ADJUSTED TRIAL BALANCE		INCOME STATEMENT		STATEMENT OF CHANGES IN OWNER'S EQUITY AND BALANCE SHEET	
	DR	CR	DR	CR	DR	CR

ACCOUNT TITLES	ADJUSTED TRIAL BALANCE DR	ADJUSTED TRIAL BALANCE CR	CLOSING ENTRIES DR	CLOSING ENTRIES CR	POST CLOSING TRIAL BALANCE DR	POST CLOSING TRIAL BALANCE CR

GENERAL JOURNAL   Page 1

DATE	ACCOUNT TITLES AND EXPLANATION	P.R.	DEBIT	CREDIT

GENERAL JOURNAL   Page 1

DATE	ACCOUNT TITLES AND EXPLANATION	P.R.	DEBIT	CREDIT

B. Holley, Capital

Rent Expense

B. Holley, Withdrawals

Salaries Expense

Income Summary

Insurance Expense

Services Revenue

Amortization Expense

EXERCISE 4–11

GENERAL JOURNAL

DATE	ACCOUNT TITLES AND EXPLANATION	P.R.	DEBIT	CREDIT

Part 1

Work Sheet

For Year Ended December 31, 19X1

ACCOUNT TITLES	UNADJUSTED TRIAL BALANCE		ADJUSTMENTS		ADJUSTED TRIAL BALANCE		INCOME STATEMENT		STATEMENT OF CHANGES IN OWNER'S EQUITY AND BALANCE SHEET	
	DR	CR	DR	CR	DR	CR	DR	CR	DR	CR

GENERAL JOURNAL   Page 1

DATE	ACCOUNT TITLES AND EXPLANATION	P.R.	DEBIT	CREDIT

Name _____

Part 3

Part 4

Part 5

Part 1

ACCOUNT TITLES	UNADJUSTED TRIAL BALANCE		ADJUSTMENTS		ADJUSTED TRIAL BALANCE		INCOME STATEMENT		STATEMENT OF CHANGES IN OWNER'S EQUITY AND BALANCE SHEET	
	DR	CR	DR	CR	DR	CR	DR	CR	DR	CR

GENERAL JOURNAL

Page 1

DATE	ACCOUNT TITLES AND EXPLANATION	P.R.	DEBIT	CREDIT

DATE	ACCOUNT TITLES AND EXPLANATION	P.R.	DEBIT	CREDIT

Fundamental Accounting Principles, Vol. I, 8th Can. Ed.

Part 4

Name _____

DOC'S DELIVERY SERVICE
Income Statement
For Year Ended December 31, 1996

DOC'S DELIVERY SERVICE
Statement of Changes in Owner's Equity
For Year Ended December 31, 1996

DOC'S DELIVERY SERVICE

Balance Sheet

December 31, 1996

Cash   111

DATE	EXPLANATION	P.R.	DEBIT	CREDIT	BALANCE

Accounts Receivable   Account No. 112

DATE	EXPLANATION	P.R.	DEBIT	CREDIT	BALANCE

Prepaid Insurance   Account No. 113

DATE	EXPLANATION	P.R.	DEBIT	CREDIT	BALANCE

Office Supplies   Account No. 114

DATE	EXPLANATION	P.R.	DEBIT	CREDIT	BALANCE

Prepaid Rent   Account No. 115

DATE	EXPLANATION	P.R.	DEBIT	CREDIT	BALANCE

Office Equipment — Account No. 131

DATE	EXPLANATION	P.R.	DEBIT	CREDIT	BALANCE

Accumulated Amortization, Office Equipment — Account No. 132

DATE	EXPLANATION	P.R.	DEBIT	CREDIT	BALANCE

Delivery Equipment — Account No. 133

DATE	EXPLANATION	P.R.	DEBIT	CREDIT	BALANCE

Accumulated Amortization, Delivery Equipment — Account No. 134

DATE	EXPLANATION	P.R.	DEBIT	CREDIT	BALANCE

Accounts Payable — Account No. 211

DATE	EXPLANATION	P.R.	DEBIT	CREDIT	BALANCE

Rent Payable   Account No. 212

DATE	EXPLANATION	P.R.	DEBIT	CREDIT	BALANCE

Salaries and Wages Payable   Account No. 213

DATE	EXPLANATION	P.R.	DEBIT	CREDIT	BALANCE

Unearned Delivery Service Revenue   Account No. 214

DATE	EXPLANATION	P.R.	DEBIT	CREDIT	BALANCE

Mark Welby, Capital   Account No. 311

DATE	EXPLANATION	P.R.	DEBIT	CREDIT	BALANCE

Mark Welby, Withdrawals   Account No. 312

DATE	EXPLANATION	P.R.	DEBIT	CREDIT	BALANCE

Income Summary — Account No. 313

DATE	EXPLANATION	P.R.	DEBIT	CREDIT	BALANCE

Delivery Service Revenue — Account No. 411

DATE	EXPLANATION	P.R.	DEBIT	CREDIT	BALANCE

Rent Expense — Account No. 511

DATE	EXPLANATION	P.R.	DEBIT	CREDIT	BALANCE

Telephone Supplies — Account No. 512

DATE	EXPLANATION	P.R.	DEBIT	CREDIT	BALANCE

Office Salaries Expense — Account No. 513

DATE	EXPLANATION	P.R.	DEBIT	CREDIT	BALANCE

Insurance Expense, Office Equipment   Account No. 514

DATE	EXPLANATION	P.R.	DEBIT	CREDIT	BALANCE

Office Supplies Expense   Account No. 515

DATE	EXPLANATION	P.R.	DEBIT	CREDIT	BALANCE

Amortization Expense, Office Equipment   Account No. 516

DATE	EXPLANATION	P.R.	DEBIT	CREDIT	BALANCE

Delivery Wages Expense   Account No. 517

DATE	EXPLANATION	P.R.	DEBIT	CREDIT	BALANCE

Gas, Oil, and Repairs Expense   Account No. 518

DATE	EXPLANATION	P.R.	DEBIT	CREDIT	BALANCE

	Insurance Expense, Delivery Expense				Account No. 519	
DATE	EXPLANATION	P.R.	DEBIT	CREDIT	BALANCE	

	Amortization Expense, Delivery Expense				Account No. 520	
DATE	EXPLANATION	P.R.	DEBIT	CREDIT	BALANCE	

DOC'S DELIVERY SERVICE

Post-Closing Trial Balance

December 31, 1996

Name _____

GENERAL JOURNAL

DATE	ACCOUNT TITLES AND EXPLANATION	P.R.	DEBIT	CREDIT

DATE	ACCOUNT TITLES AND EXPLANATION	P.R.	DEBIT	CREDIT

GENERAL JOURNAL

DATE	ACCOUNT TITLES AND EXPLANATION	P.R.	DEBIT	CREDIT

DATE	ACCOUNT TITLES AND EXPLANATION	P.R.	DEBIT	CREDIT

GENERAL LEDGER

Cash   Account No. 111

DATE	EXPLANATION	P.R.	DEBIT	CREDIT	BALANCE

Prepaid Insurance   Account No. 113

DATE	EXPLANATION	P.R.	DEBIT	CREDIT	BALANCE

Office Supplies   Account No. 114

DATE	EXPLANATION	P.R.	DEBIT	CREDIT	BALANCE

Automobile — Account No. 131

DATE	EXPLANATION	P.R.	DEBIT	CREDIT	BALANCE

Accumulated Amortization, Automobile — Account No. 132

DATE	EXPLANATION	P.R.	DEBIT	CREDIT	BALANCE

Salaries Payable — Account No. 213

DATE	EXPLANATION	P.R.	DEBIT	CREDIT	BALANCE

Tami Martin, Capital — Account No. 311

DATE	EXPLANATION	P.R.	DEBIT	CREDIT	BALANCE

Tami Martin, Withdrawals — Account No. 312

DATE	EXPLANATION	P.R.	DEBIT	CREDIT	BALANCE

Income Summary — Account No. 313

DATE	EXPLANATION	P.R.	DEBIT	CREDIT	BALANCE

Commissions Earned   Account No. 411

DATE	EXPLANATION	P.R.	DEBIT	CREDIT	BALANCE

Rent Expense   Account No. 511

DATE	EXPLANATION	P.R.	DEBIT	CREDIT	BALANCE

Salaries Expense   Account No. 512

DATE	EXPLANATION	P.R.	DEBIT	CREDIT	BALANCE

Gas, Oil, and Repairs Expense   Account No. 513

DATE	EXPLANATION	P.R.	DEBIT	CREDIT	BALANCE

Telephone Expense   Account No. 514

DATE	EXPLANATION	P.R.	DEBIT	CREDIT	BALANCE

Insurance Expense   Account No. 515

DATE	EXPLANATION	P.R.	DEBIT	CREDIT	BALANCE

Office Supplies Expense   Account No. 516

DATE	EXPLANATION	P.R.	DEBIT	CREDIT	BALANCE

Amortization Expense, Automobile   Account No. 517

DATE	EXPLANATION	P.R.	DEBIT	CREDIT	BALANCE

MARTIN REALTY
Work Sheet
For Month Ended May 31, 1996

ACCOUNT TITLES	TRIAL BALANCE		ADJUSTMENTS		ADJUSTED TRIAL BALANCE		INCOME STATEMENT		STATEMENT OF CHANGES IN OWNERS'S EQUITY OR BALANCE SHEET	
	DR.	CR.	DR.	CR.	DR.	CR.	DR.	CR.	DR.	CR.

MARTIN REALTY
Work Sheet
For Month Ended June 30, 1996

ACCOUNT TITLES	TRIAL BALANCE		ADJUSTMENTS		ADJUSTED TRIAL BALANCE		INCOME STATEMENT		STATEMENT OF CHANGES IN OWNERS'S EQUITY OR BALANCE SHEET	
	DR.	CR.	DR.	CR.	DR.	CR.	DR.	CR.	DR.	CR.

MARTIN REALTY

Income Statement

For Year Ended December 31, 1996

MARTIN REALTY

Statement of Changes in Owner's Equity

For Year Ended December 31, 1996

MARTIN REALTY

Balance Sheet

May 31, 1996

MARTIN REALTY

Post-Closing Trial Balance

May 31, 1996

MARTIN REALTY

Income Statement

For Month Ended June 30,1996

MARTIN REALTY

Statement of Changes in Owner's Equity

For Month Ended June 30, 1996

MARTIN REALTY

Balance Sheet

June 30, 1996

MARTIN REALTY

Post-Closing Trial Balance

June 30, 1996

Name _____

GENERAL JOURNAL

Page 1

DATE	ACCOUNT TITLES AND EXPLANATION	P.R.	DEBIT	CREDIT

Part 5

Name _____

GENERAL JOURNAL

DATE	ACCOUNT TITLES AND EXPLANATION	P.R.	DEBIT	CREDIT

Part 1

GENERAL LEDGER

Cash   Account No. 101

DATE	ACCOUNT TITLES AND EXPLANATION	P.R.	DEBIT	CREDIT	BALANCE

Accounts Receivable   Account No. 106

DATE	ACCOUNT TITLES AND EXPLANATION	P.R.	DEBIT	CREDIT	BALANCE

Office Supplies   Account No. 124

DATE	ACCOUNT TITLES AND EXPLANATION	P.R.	DEBIT	CREDIT	BALANCE

Prepaid Insurance   Account No. 128

DATE	ACCOUNT TITLES AND EXPLANATION	P.R.	DEBIT	CREDIT	BALANCE

Computer Equipment   Account No. 167

DATE	ACCOUNT TITLES AND EXPLANATION	P.R.	DEBIT	CREDIT	BALANCE

Accumulated Amortization, Computer Equipment   Account No. 168

DATE	ACCOUNT TITLES AND EXPLANATION	P.R.	DEBIT	CREDIT	BALANCE

Salaries Payable   Account No. 209

DATE	ACCOUNT TITLES AND EXPLANATION	P.R.	DEBIT	CREDIT	BALANCE

_____, Capital   Account No. 301

DATE	ACCOUNT TITLES AND EXPLANATION	P.R.	DEBIT	CREDIT	BALANCE

_____, Withdrawals   Account No. 302

DATE	ACCOUNT TITLES AND EXPLANATION	P.R.	DEBIT	CREDIT	BALANCE

Commissions Earned   Account No. 405

DATE	ACCOUNT TITLES AND EXPLANATION	P.R.	DEBIT	CREDIT	BALANCE

Amortization Expense, Computer Equipment   Account No. 612

DATE	ACCOUNT TITLES AND EXPLANATION	P.R.	DEBIT	CREDIT	BALANCE

Salaries Expense   Account No. 622

DATE	ACCOUNT TITLES AND EXPLANATION	P.R.	DEBIT	CREDIT	BALANCE

Insurance Expense   Account No. 637

DATE	ACCOUNT TITLES AND EXPLANATION	P.R.	DEBIT	CREDIT	BALANCE

Rent Expense   Account No. 640

DATE	ACCOUNT TITLES AND EXPLANATION	P.R.	DEBIT	CREDIT	BALANCE

Office Supplies Expense   Account No. 650

DATE	ACCOUNT TITLES AND EXPLANATION	P.R.	DEBIT	CREDIT	BALANCE

Repairs Expense   Account No. 684

DATE	ACCOUNT TITLES AND EXPLANATION	P.R.	DEBIT	CREDIT	BALANCE

Telephone Expense   Account No. 688

DATE	ACCOUNT TITLES AND EXPLANATION	P.R.	DEBIT	CREDIT	BALANCE

Income Summary   Account No. 901

DATE	ACCOUNT TITLES AND EXPLANATION	P.R.	DEBIT	CREDIT	BALANCE

	ACCOUNT TITLES	UNADJUSTED TRIAL BALANCE		ADJUSTMENTS	
		DR.	CR.	DR.	CR.
1	Cash				
2	Office Supplies				
3	Prepaid Insurance				
4	Automobiles				
5	Accumulated amortization,				
6	automobiles				
7	Office equipment				
8	Accumulated amortization,				
9	Office equipment				
10	Accounts payable				
11	Interest payable				
12	Salaries payable				
13	Unearned fees				
14	Long-term notes payable				
15	Charlie Griffin, capital				
16	Charlie Griffin, withdrawals				
17	Fees earned				
18	Amortization expense, automobiles				
19	Amortization expense,				
20	office equipment				
21	Salaries expense				
22	Interest expense				
23	Insurance expense				
24	Rent expense				
25	Office supplies expense				
26	Gas, oil, and repairs expense				
27	Telephone expense				
28	Totals				
29	Net income				
30	Totals				
31					
32					
33					
34					
35					
36					
37					

ADJUSTED TRIAL BALANCE		INCOME STATEMENT		STATEMENT OF CHANGES IN OWNER'S EQUITY OR BALANCE SHEET		
DR.	CR.	DR.	CR.	DR.	CR.	
						1
						2
						3
						4
						5
						6
						7
						8
						9
						10
						11
						12
						13
						14
						15
						16
						17
						18
						19
						20
						21
						22
						23
						24
						25
						26
						27
						28
						29
						30
						31
						32
						33
						34
						35
						36
						37

Account Titles	Unadjusted Trial Balance		Adjustments		Adjusted Trial Balance	

Part 2

PROBLEM 4–8 (Continued)

GENERAL JOURNAL

Page 1

DATE	ACCOUNT TITLES AND EXPLANATION	P.R.	DEBIT	CREDIT

Parts 3 and 4

DATE	ACCOUNT TITLES AND EXPLANATION	P.R.	DEBIT	CREDIT

DATE	ACCOUNT TITLES AND EXPLANATION	P.R.	DEBIT	CREDIT

GENERAL JOURNAL

DATE	ACCOUNT TITLES AND EXPLANATION	P.R.	DEBIT	CREDIT

DATE	ACCOUNT TITLES AND EXPLANATION	P.R.	DEBIT	CREDIT

       Fundamental Accounting Principles, Vol. I, 8th Can. Ed.

GENERAL JOURNAL

DATE	ACCOUNT TITLES AND EXPLANATION	P.R.	DEBIT	CREDIT

GENERAL LEDGER

Cash   Account No. 101

DATE	EXPLANATION	P.R.	DEBIT	CREDIT	BALANCE
1996 Dec. 31	Balance				27 2 3 0 00

Accounts Receivable   Account No. 106

DATE	EXPLANATION	P.R.	DEBIT	CREDIT	BALANCE
1996 Dec. 31	Balance				1 9 0 0 00

Computer Supplies   Account No. 126

DATE	EXPLANATION	P.R.	DEBIT	CREDIT	BALANCE
1996 Dec. 31	Balance				4 8 0 00

Prepaid Insurance   Account No. 128

DATE	EXPLANATION	P.R.	DEBIT	CREDIT	BALANCE
1996 Dec. 31	Balance				1 0 8 0 00

Prepaid Rent   Account No. 131

DATE	EXPLANATION	P.R.	DEBIT	CREDIT	BALANCE
1996 Dec. 31	Balance				7 5 0 00

Office Equipment   Account No. 163

DATE	EXPLANATION	P.R.	DEBIT	CREDIT	BALANCE
1996 Dec. 31	Balance				6 0 0 0 00

Accumulated Amortization, Office Equipment — Account No. 164

DATE	EXPLANATION	P.R.	DEBIT	CREDIT	BALANCE
1996 Dec. 31	Balance				5 0 0 00

Computer Equipment — Account No. 167

DATE	EXPLANATION	P.R.	DEBIT	CREDIT	BALANCE
1996 Dec. 31	Balance				12 0 0 0 00

Accumulated Amortization, Computer Equipment — Account No. 168

DATE	EXPLANATION	P.R.	DEBIT	CREDIT	BALANCE
1996 Dec. 31	Balance				7 5 0 00

Accounts Payable — Account No. 201

DATE	EXPLANATION	P.R.	DEBIT	CREDIT	BALANCE
1996 Dec. 31	Balance				7 7 0 00

Wages Payable — Account No. 210

DATE	EXPLANATION	P.R.	DEBIT	CREDIT	BALANCE
1996 Dec. 31	Balance				5 0 0 00

Unearned Computer Fees — Account No. 233

DATE	EXPLANATION	P.R.	DEBIT	CREDIT	BALANCE
1996 Dec. 31	Balance				1 0 0 0 00

Tracy Green, Capital — Account No. 301

DATE	EXPLANATION	P.R.	DEBIT	CREDIT	BALANCE
1996 Dec. 31	Balance				48 0 0 0 00

Tracy Green, Withdrawals — Account No. 302

DATE	EXPLANATION	P.R.	DEBIT	CREDIT	BALANCE
19X1 Dec. 31	Balance				6 1 5 0 00

Computer Services Revenue — Account No. 403

DATE	EXPLANATION	P.R.	DEBIT	CREDIT	BALANCE
19X1 Dec. 31	Balance				17 4 0 0 00

Amortization Expense, Office Equipment — Account No. 612

DATE	EXPLANATION	P.R.	DEBIT	CREDIT	BALANCE
19X1 Dec. 31	Balance				5 0 0 00

Amortization Expense, Computer Equipment — Account No. 613

DATE	EXPLANATION	P.R.	DEBIT	CREDIT	BALANCE
19X1 Dec. 31	Balance				7 5 0 00

Wages Expense   Account No. 623

DATE	EXPLANATION	P.R.	DEBIT	CREDIT	BALANCE
1996 Dec. 31	Balance				3 8 7 5 00

Insurance Expense   Account No. 637

DATE	EXPLANATION	P.R.	DEBIT	CREDIT	BALANCE
1996 Dec. 31	Balance				3 6 0 00

Rent Expense   Account No. 640

DATE	EXPLANATION	P.R.	DEBIT	CREDIT	BALANCE
1996 Dec. 31	Balance				2 2 5 0 00

Computer Supplies Expense   Account No. 652

DATE	EXPLANATION	P.R.	DEBIT	CREDIT	BALANCE
1996 Dec. 31	Balance				1 8 1 0 00

Advertising Expense   Account No. 655

DATE	EXPLANATION	P.R.	DEBIT	CREDIT	BALANCE
1996 Dec. 31	Balance				1 9 4 0 00

Mileage Expense | Account No. 676

DATE	EXPLANATION	P.R.	DEBIT	CREDIT	BALANCE
1996 Dec. 31	Balance				475 00

Miscellaneous Expenses | Account No. 677

DATE	EXPLANATION	P.R.	DEBIT	CREDIT	BALANCE
1996 Dec. 31	Balance				500 00

Repairs Expense, Computer | Account No. 684

DATE	EXPLANATION	P.R.	DEBIT	CREDIT	BALANCE
1996 Dec. 31	Balance				870 00

Income Summary | Account No. 901

DATE	EXPLANATION	P.R.	DEBIT	CREDIT	BALANCE

EMERALD COMPUTER SERVICES

Post-Closing Trial Balance

December 31, 1996

GENERAL JOURNAL   Page 1

DATE	ACCOUNT TITLES AND EXPLANATION	P.R.	DEBIT	CREDIT

DATE	ACCOUNT TITLES AND EXPLANATION	P.R.	DEBIT	CREDIT

PIPER'S PLUMBING AND HEATING
Income Statement
For Year Ended December 31, 1996

PIPER'S PLUMBING AND HEATING
Statement of Changes in Owner's Equity
For Year Ended December 31, 1996

PIPER'S PLUMBING AND HEATING

Balance Sheet

December 31, 1996

Part 7

PIPER'S PLUMBING AND HEATING
Post-Closing Trial Balance
December 31, 1996

Part 8

COMPREHENSIVE PROBLEM
Piper's Plumbing and Heating (Continued)
Parts 1, 2, 4 and 6

GENERAL LEDGER

Cash   Account No. 101

DATE	EXPLANATION	P.R.	DEBIT	CREDIT	BALANCE
Nov. 30	Balance	✓			17 0 0 0 00

Office Supplies   Account No. 124

DATE	EXPLANATION	P.R.	DEBIT	CREDIT	BALANCE
Nov. 30	Balance	✓			9 4 0 0 00

Repair Supplies   Account No. 126

DATE	EXPLANATION	P.R.	DEBIT	CREDIT	BALANCE
Nov. 30	Balance	✓			86 5 0 0 00

Prepaid Insurance   Account No. 128

DATE	EXPLANATION	P.R.	DEBIT	CREDIT	BALANCE
Nov. 30	Balance	✓			2 4 0 0 00

Trucks — Account No. 153

DATE	EXPLANATION	P.R.	DEBIT	CREDIT	BALANCE
Nov. 30	Balance	✓			82 0 0 0 00

Accumulated Depreciation, Trucks — Account No. 154

DATE	EXPLANATION	P.R.	DEBIT	CREDIT	BALANCE
Nov. 30	Balance	✓			40 0 0 0 00

Building — Account No. 173

DATE	EXPLANATION	P.R.	DEBIT	CREDIT	BALANCE
Nov. 30	Balance	✓			185 0 0 0 00

Accumulated Amortization, Building — Account No. 174

DATE	EXPLANATION	P.R.	DEBIT	CREDIT	BALANCE
Nov. 30	Balance	✓			32 0 0 0 00

Accounts Payable — Account No. 201

DATE	EXPLANATION	P.R.	DEBIT	CREDIT	BALANCE
Nov. 30	Balance	✓			13 5 0 0 00

COMPREHENSIVE PROBLEM
Piper's Plumbing and Heating (Continued)

Wages Payable   Account No. 210

DATE	EXPLANATION	P.R.	DEBIT	CREDIT	BALANCE
Nov. 30	Balance	✔			- 0 -

Unearned Heating Fees   Account No. 233

DATE	EXPLANATION	P.R.	DEBIT	CREDIT	BALANCE
Nov. 30	Balance	✔			3 7 0 0 00

Bill Piper, Capital   Account No. 301

DATE	EXPLANATION	P.R.	DEBIT	CREDIT	BALANCE
Nov. 30	Balance	✔			174 6 0 0 00

Bill Piper, Withdrawals   Account No. 302

DATE	EXPLANATION	P.R.	DEBIT	CREDIT	BALANCE
Nov. 30	Balance	✔			30 0 0 0 00

Plumbing Fees Earned Account No. 401

DATE	EXPLANATION	P.R.	DEBIT	CREDIT	BALANCE
Nov. 30	Balance	✔			180 0 0 0 00

Heating Fees Earned Account No. 402

DATE	EXPLANATION	P.R.	DEBIT	CREDIT	BALANCE
Nov. 30	Balance	✔			95 0 0 0 00

Amortization Expense, Building Account No. 606

DATE	EXPLANATION	P.R.	DEBIT	CREDIT	BALANCE
Nov. 30	Balance	✔			- 0 -

Amortization Expense, Trucks Account No. 611

DATE	EXPLANATION	P.R.	DEBIT	CREDIT	BALANCE
Nov. 30	Balance	✔			- 0 -

Wages Expense   Account No. 623

DATE	EXPLANATION	P.R.	DEBIT	CREDIT	BALANCE
Nov. 30	Balance	✓			65 0 0 0 00

Insurance Expense   Account No. 637

DATE	EXPLANATION	P.R.	DEBIT	CREDIT	BALANCE
Nov. 30	Balance	✓			- 0 -

Office Supplies Expense   Account No. 650

DATE	EXPLANATION	P.R.	DEBIT	CREDIT	BALANCE
Nov. 30	Balance	✓			- 0 -

Repair Supplies Expense   Account No. 652

DATE	EXPLANATION	P.R.	DEBIT	CREDIT	BALANCE
Nov. 30	Balance	✓			- 0 -

Gas, Oil, and Repairs Expense   Account No. 669

DATE	EXPLANATION	P.R.	DEBIT	CREDIT	BALANCE
Nov. 30	Balance	✓			13 5 0 0 00

General and Administrative Expenses   Account No. 672

DATE	EXPLANATION	P.R.	DEBIT	CREDIT	BALANCE
Nov. 30	Balance	✓			48 0 0 0 00

Income Summary   Account No. 901

DATE	EXPLANATION	P.R.	DEBIT	CREDIT	BALANCE

EXERCISE 5–2

GENERAL JOURNAL

DATE	ACCOUNT TITLES AND EXPLANATION	P.R.	DEBIT	CREDIT

Name _____

GENERAL JOURNAL

Page 1

DATE	ACCOUNT TITLES AND EXPLANATION	P.R.	DEBIT	CREDIT

DATE	ACCOUNT TITLES AND EXPLANATION	P.R.	DEBIT	CREDIT

Name _____

GENERAL JOURNAL   Page 1

DATE	ACCOUNT TITLES AND EXPLANATION	P.R.	DEBIT	CREDIT

GENERAL LEDGER

Merchandise Inventory   Account No. 119

DATE	EXPLANATION	P.R.	DEBIT	CREDIT	BALANCE

GENERAL JOURNAL

DATE	ACCOUNT TITLES AND EXPLANATION	P.R.	DEBIT	CREDIT

Page 2

DATE	ACCOUNT TITLES AND EXPLANATION	P.R.	DEBIT	CREDIT

GENERAL LEDGER

Merchandise Inventory   Account No. 119

DATE	EXPLANATION	P.R.	DEBIT	CREDIT	BALANCE

           Fundamental Accounting Principles, Vol. I, 8th Can. Ed.

JOHNSON'S NEWSTAND
Work Sheet
For Year Ended December 31

ACCOUNT TITLES	UNADJUSTED TRIAL BALANCE		ADJUSTMENTS		INCOME STATEMENT		STATEMENT OF CHANGES IN OWNER'S EQUITY AND BALANCE SHEET	
	DR	CR	DR	CR	DR	CR	DR	CR

Name _____

GENERAL JOURNAL

Page 1

DATE	ACCOUNT TITLES AND EXPLANATION	P.R.	DEBIT	CREDIT

DATE	ACCOUNT TITLES AND EXPLANATION	P.R.	DEBIT	CREDIT

Page 1

DATE	ACCOUNT TITLES AND EXPLANATION	P.R.	DEBIT	CREDIT

GENERAL JOURNAL

DATE	ACCOUNT TITLES AND EXPLANATION	P.R.	DEBIT	CREDIT

GENERAL JOURNAL

DATE	ACCOUNT TITLES AND EXPLANATION	P.R.	DEBIT	CREDIT

GENERAL JOURNAL

DATE	ACCOUNT TITLES AND EXPLANATION	P.R.	DEBIT	CREDIT

Merchandise Inventory

DATE	EXPLANATION	P.R.	DEBIT	CREDIT	BALANCE

GENERAL JOURNAL

DATE	ACCOUNT TITLES AND EXPLANATION	P.R.	DEBIT	CREDIT

	ACCOUNT TITLES	TRIAL BALANCE	
		DR.	CR.
1	Cash		
2	Merchandise inventory		
3	Store supplies		
4	Office supplies		
5	Prepaid insurance		
6	Store equipment		
7	Accumulated amortization, store equipment		
8	Office equipment		
9	Accumulated amortization, office equipment		
10	Accounts payable		
11	, capital		
12	, withdrawal		
13	Sales		
14	Sales returns and allowances		
15	Sales discounts		
16	Purchases		
17	Purchases returns and allowances		
18	Purchases discounts		
19	Transportation-in		
20	Sales salaries expense		
21	Rent expense, selling space		
22	Advertising expense		
23	Store supplies expense		
24	Amortization expense, store equipment		
25	Office salaries expense		
26	Rent expense, office space		
27	Office supplies expense		
28	Insurance expense		
29	Amortization expense, office equipment		
30			
31			
32			
33			
34			
35			

ADJUSTMENTS		INCOME STATEMENT		STATEMENT OF CHANGES IN OWNER'S EQUITY OR BALANCE SHEET		
DR.	CR.	DR.	CR.	DR.	CR.	
						1
						2
						3
						4
						5
						6
						7
						8
						9
						10
						11
						12
						13
						14
						15
						16
						17
						18
						19
						20
						21
						22
						23
						24
						25
						26
						27
						28
						29
						30
						31
						32
						33
						34
						35

DATE	ACCOUNT TITLES AND EXPLANATION	P.R.	DEBIT	CREDIT

Merchandise Inventory

DATE	EXPLANATION	P.R.	DEBIT	CREDIT	BALANCE

Part 1

Part 5

Part 1

GENERAL JOURNAL

DATE	ACCOUNT TITLES AND EXPLANATION	P.R.	DEBIT	CREDIT

DATE	ACCOUNT TITLES AND EXPLANATION	P.R.	DEBIT	CREDIT

	ACCOUNT TITLES	TRIAL BALANCE	
		DR.	CR.
1	Cash		
2	Accounts receivable		
3	Merchandise inventory		
4	Store supplies		
5	Office supplies		
6	Prepaid insurance		
7	Store equipment		
8	Accumulated amortization, store equipment		
9	Office equipment		
10	Accumulated amortization, office equipment		
11	Accounts payable		
12	Salaries payable		
13	_____, capital		
14	_____, withdrawal		
15	Sales		
16	Sales returns and allowances		
17	Purchases		
18	Purchases returns and allowances		
19	Purchases discounts		
20	Transportation-in		
21	Sales salaries expense		
22	Rent expense, selling space		
23	Store supplies expense		
24	Amortization expense, store equipment		
25	Office salaries expense		
26	Rent expense, office space		
27	Office supplies expense		
28	Insurance expense		
29	Amortization expense, office equipment		
30			
31			
32			
33			
34			
35			

ADJUSTMENTS				INCOME STATEMENT				STATEMENT OF CHANGES IN OWNER'S EQUITY OR BALANCE SHEET				
DR.		CR.		DR.		CR.		DR.		CR.		
												1
												2
												3
												4
												5
												6
												7
												8
												9
												10
												11
												12
												13
												14
												15
												16
												17
												18
												19
												20
												21
												22
												23
												24
												25
												26
												27
												28
												29
												30
												31
												32
												33
												34
												35

DATE	ACCOUNT TITLES AND EXPLANATION	P.R.	DEBIT	CREDIT

DATE	ACCOUNT TITLES AND EXPLANATION	P.R.	DEBIT	CREDIT

GENERAL JOURNAL

DATE	ACCOUNT TITLES AND EXPLANATION	P.R.	DEBIT	CREDIT

DATE	ACCOUNT TITLES AND EXPLANATION	P.R.	DEBIT	CREDIT

DATE	ACCOUNT TITLES AND EXPLANATION	P.R.	DEBIT	CREDIT

DATE	ACCOUNT TITLES AND EXPLANATION	P.R.	DEBIT	CREDIT

GENERAL LEDGER

| Cash Account | | | | | | Account No. 101 |

DATE	EXPLANATION	P.R.	DEBIT	CREDIT	BALANCE
1996 Dec. 31	Balance				27 2 3 0 00

Account Receivable—Alpha Printing Co. Account No. 106.1

DATE	EXPLANATION	P.R.	DEBIT	CREDIT	BALANCE

Account Receivable—Bravo Productions Account No. 106.2

DATE	EXPLANATION	P.R.	DEBIT	CREDIT	BALANCE

Account Receivable—Charles Company Account No. 106.3

DATE	EXPLANATION	P.R.	DEBIT	CREDIT	BALANCE
1996 Dec. 31	Balance				9 0 0 00

Account Receivable—Delta Fixtures, Inc. Account No. 106.4

DATE	EXPLANATION	P.R.	DEBIT	CREDIT	BALANCE

Account Receivable—Echo Canyon Ranch Account No. 106.5

DATE	EXPLANATION	P.R.	DEBIT	CREDIT	BALANCE

Account Receivable—Fox Run Estates   Account No. 106.6

DATE	EXPLANATION	P.R.	DEBIT	CREDIT	BALANCE
1996 Dec. 31	Balance				1 0 0 0 00

Account Receivable—Golf Course Designs, Inc.   Account No. 106.7

DATE	EXPLANATION	P.R.	DEBIT	CREDIT	BALANCE

Account Receivable—Hotel Pollo del Mar   Account No. 106.8

DATE	EXPLANATION	P.R.	DEBIT	CREDIT	BALANCE

Account Receivable—Indiana M Co.   Account No. 106.9

DATE	EXPLANATION	P.R.	DEBIT	CREDIT	BALANCE

Computer Supplies   Account No. 126

DATE	EXPLANATION	P.R.	DEBIT	CREDIT	BALANCE
1996 Dec. 31	Balance				4 8 0 00

SERIAL PROBLEM
Emerald Computer Services (Continued)

	Prepaid Insurance				Account No. 128

DATE	EXPLANATION	P.R.	DEBIT	CREDIT	BALANCE
1996 Dec. 31	Balance				1 0 8 0 00

	Prepaid Rent				Account No. 131

DATE	EXPLANATION	P.R.	DEBIT	CREDIT	BALANCE
1996 Dec. 31	Balance				7 5 0 00

	Office Equipment				Account No. 163

DATE	EXPLANATION	P.R.	DEBIT	CREDIT	BALANCE
1996 Dec. 31	Balance				6 0 0 0 00

	Accumulated Amortization, Office Equipment				Account No. 164

DATE	EXPLANATION	P.R.	DEBIT	CREDIT	BALANCE
1996 Dec. 31	Balance				5 0 0 00

	Computer Equipment				Account No. 167

DATE	EXPLANATION	P.R.	DEBIT	CREDIT	BALANCE
1996 Dec. 31	Balance				12 0 0 0 00

Accumulated Amortization, Computer Equipment					Account No. 168	
DATE	EXPLANATION	P.R.	DEBIT	CREDIT	BALANCE	
1996 Dec. 31	Balance				7 5 0 00	

Accounts Payable					Account No. 201	
DATE	EXPLANATION	P.R.	DEBIT	CREDIT	BALANCE	
1996 Dec. 31	Balance				7 7 0 00	

Wages Payable					Account No. 210	
DATE	EXPLANATION	P.R.	DEBIT	CREDIT	BALANCE	
1996 Dec. 31	Balance				5 0 0 00	

Unearned Computer Fees   Account No. 233

DATE	EXPLANATION	P.R.	DEBIT	CREDIT	BALANCE
1996 Dec. 31	Balance				1 0 0 0 00

Tracy Green, Capital   Account No. 301

DATE	EXPLANATION	P.R.	DEBIT	CREDIT	BALANCE
1996 Dec. 31	Balance				45 9 2 0 00

Tracy Green, Withdrawals   Account No. 302

DATE	EXPLANATION	P.R.	DEBIT	CREDIT	BALANCE

Computer Services Revenue   Account No. 403

DATE	EXPLANATION	P.R.	DEBIT	CREDIT	BALANCE

		Sales				Account No. 413	
DATE	EXPLANATION			P.R.	DEBIT	CREDIT	BALANCE

		Sales Returns and Allowances				Account No. 414	
DATE	EXPLANATION			P.R.	DEBIT	CREDIT	BALANCE

		Sales Discounts				Account No. 415	
DATE	EXPLANATION			P.R.	DEBIT	CREDIT	BALANCE

		Purchases				Account No. 505	
DATE	EXPLANATION			P.R.	DEBIT	CREDIT	BALANCE

		Purchases Returns and Allowances				Account No. 506	
DATE	EXPLANATION			P.R.	DEBIT	CREDIT	BALANCE

		Purchases Discounts				Account No. 507	
DATE	EXPLANATION			P.R.	DEBIT	CREDIT	BALANCE

SERIAL PROBLEM
Emerald Computer Services (Continued)

Transportation-In — Account No. 508

DATE	EXPLANATION	P.R.	DEBIT	CREDIT	BALANCE

Amortization Expense, Office Equipment — Account No. 612

DATE	EXPLANATION	P.R.	DEBIT	CREDIT	BALANCE

Amortization Expense, Computer Equipment — Account No. 613

DATE	EXPLANATION	P.R.	DEBIT	CREDIT	BALANCE

Wages Expense — Account No. 623

DATE	EXPLANATION	P.R.	DEBIT	CREDIT	BALANCE

Insurance Expense — Account No. 637

DATE	EXPLANATION	P.R.	DEBIT	CREDIT	BALANCE

Rent Expense — Account No. 640

DATE	EXPLANATION	P.R.	DEBIT	CREDIT	BALANCE

Computer Supplies Expense   Account No. 652

DATE	EXPLANATION	P.R.	DEBIT	CREDIT	BALANCE

Advertising Expense   Account No. 655

DATE	EXPLANATION	P.R.	DEBIT	CREDIT	BALANCE

Mileage Expense   Account No. 676

DATE	EXPLANATION	P.R.	DEBIT	CREDIT	BALANCE

Miscellaneous Expenses   Account No. 677

DATE	EXPLANATION	P.R.	DEBIT	CREDIT	BALANCE

Repairs Expense, Computer   Account No. 684

DATE	EXPLANATION	P.R.	DEBIT	CREDIT	BALANCE

EMERALD COMPUTER SERVICES
Adjusted Trial Balance
March 31, 19X2

ACCOUNT TITLES	UNADJUSTED TRIAL BALANCE		ADJUSTMENTS		ADJUSTED TRIAL BALANCE	
	DR	CR	DR	CR	DR	CR

ACCOUNT TITLES	UNADJUSTED TRIAL BALANCE		ADJUSTMENTS		ADJUSTED TRIAL BALANCE	
	DR	CR	DR	CR	DR	CR

EMERALD COMPUTER SERVICES

Income Statement

For Three Months Ended March 31, 1997

EMERALD COMPUTER SERVICES

Statement of Changes in Owner's Equity

For Three Months Ended March 31, 1997

EMERALD COMPUTER SERVICES

Balance Sheet

March 31, 1997

Name _____

SALES JOURNAL

DATE	ACCOUNT DEBITED	INVOICE NUMBER	P.R.	AMOUNT

CASH RECEIPTS JOURNAL

DATE	ACCOUNT CREDITED	EXPLANATION	P.R.	OTHER ACCOUNTS CREDIT	ACCOUNTS RECEIVABLE CREDIT	SALES CREDIT	SALES DISCOUNTS DEBIT	CASH DEBIT

EXERCISE 6-3

PURCHASES JOURNAL

DATE	ACCOUNT	DATE OF INVOICE	TERMS	P.R.	PURCHASES DEBIT	OFFICE SUPPLIES DEBIT	OTHER ACCOUNTS DEBIT	ACCOUNTS PAYABLE CREDIT

EXERCISE 6-4

CASH DISBURSEMENTS JOURNAL

DATE	CH. NO.	PAYEE	ACCOUNT DEBITED	P.R.	OTHER ACCOUNTS DEBIT	ACCOUNTS PAYABLE DEBIT	PURCHASES DISCOUNTS CREDIT	CASH CREDIT

EXERCISE 6–6   ACCOUNTS RECEIVABLE LEDGER

Sandy Ford	Don Holly	Bud Smith

Part 2   GENERAL LEDGER

Accounts Receivable	Sales	Sales Returns and Allowances

Part 3

ACCOUNTS RECEIVABLE LEDGER

Adrian Carr

Lisa Mack

Jay Newton

Kathy Olivas

GENERAL JOURNAL

Page 1

DATE	ACCOUNT TITLES AND EXPLANATION	P.R.	DEBIT	CREDIT

GENERAL LEDGER

Accounts Receivable	Sales

GST Payable	PST Payable

GENERAL LEDGER

Cash	Accounts Payable	Sales Discounts

Accounts Receivable	Notes Payable	Purchases

Prepaid Insurance	Sales	Purchases Returns and Allowances

Store Equipment	Sales Returns and Allowances	Purchases Discounts

ACCOUNTS RECEIVABLE LEDGER

Wayne Day	Jack Heinz	Trudy Stone

ACCOUNTS PAYABLE LEDGER

Frasier Corp.	McGraw Company	Sultan, Inc.

PURCHASES JOURNAL

Page 3

DATE	ACCOUNT	DATE OF INVOICE	TERMS	P.R.	PURCHASES DEBIT	OTHER ACCOUNTS DEBIT	ACCOUNTS PAYABLE CREDIT

CASH DISBURSEMENTS JOURNAL

Page 3

DATE	CH. NO.	PAYEE	ACCOUNT DEBITED	P.R.	OTHER ACCOUNTS DEBIT	ACCOUNTS PAYABLE DEBIT	PURCHASES DISCOUNTS CREDIT	CASH CREDIT

GENERAL JOURNAL   Page 3

DATE	ACCOUNT TITLES AND EXPLANATION	P.R.	DEBIT	CREDIT

GENERAL LEDGER

Cash   Account No. 101

DATE	EXPLANATION	P.R.	DEBIT	CREDIT	BALANCE

Office Supplies   Account No. 124

DATE	EXPLANATION	P.R.	DEBIT	CREDIT	BALANCE

Store Supplies   Account No. 125

DATE	EXPLANATION	P.R.	DEBIT	CREDIT	BALANCE

Store Equipment   Account No. 165

DATE	EXPLANATION	P.R.	DEBIT	CREDIT	BALANCE

Accounts Payable   Account No. 201

DATE	EXPLANATION	P.R.	DEBIT	CREDIT	BALANCE

Long-Term Notes Payable   Account No. 251

DATE	EXPLANATION	P.R.	DEBIT	CREDIT	BALANCE

Purchases   Account No. 505

DATE	EXPLANATION	P.R.	DEBIT	CREDIT	BALANCE

Purchases Returns and Allowances   Account No. 506

DATE	EXPLANATION	P.R.	DEBIT	CREDIT	BALANCE

Purchases Discounts   Account No. 507

DATE	EXPLANATION	P.R.	DEBIT	CREDIT	BALANCE

Sales Salaries Expense   Account No. 621

DATE	EXPLANATION	P.R.	DEBIT	CREDIT	BALANCE

	Advertising Expense					Account No. 655
DATE	EXPLANATION	P.R.	DEBIT	CREDIT	BALANCE	

ACCOUNTS PAYABLE LEDGER

NAME   Cooper's Supply

ADDRESS   Cranston, Illinois

DATE	EXPLANATION	P.R.	DEBIT	CREDIT	BALANCE

NAME   Flott Company

ADDRESS   Derby, Ohio

DATE	EXPLANATION	P.R.	DEBIT	CREDIT	BALANCE

NAME   Sprague Company

ADDRESS   Gosport, Indiana

DATE	EXPLANATION	P.R.	DEBIT	CREDIT	BALANCE

NAME   Whitewater, Inc.

ADDRESS   32nd and Maple

DATE	EXPLANATION	P.R.	DEBIT	CREDIT	BALANCE

SALES JOURNAL

Page 3

DATE		ACCOUNT DEBITED	INVOICE NUMBER	P.R.	AMOUNT
Dec.	6	Marge Craig	913	✓	3 3 0 0 00
	12	Ambrose Fielder	914	✓	3 6 5 0 00
	15	Amy Oakley	915	✓	3 1 0 0 00

PURCHASES JOURNAL

Page 2

DATE		ACCOUNT	DATE OF INVOICE	TERMS	P.R.	PURCHASES DEBIT	OFFICE SUPPLIES DEBIT	OTHER ACCOUNTS DEBIT	ACCOUNTS PAYABLE CREDIT
Dec.	2	Weathers Company	12/ 2	2/10, n/60		3 2 0 0 00			3 2 0 0 00
	5	Gray Supply Co.	12/ 3	n/10 EOM		1 3 0 0 00			1 3 0 0 00
	15	Weathers Company	12/15	2/10, n/60		3 9 9 0 00			3 9 9 0 00
	15	Shunshine Company	12/15	2/10, n/60		2 6 5 0 00			2 6 5 0 00

CASH RECEIPTS JOURNAL

Page 3

DATE		ACCOUNT CREDITED	EXPLANATION	P.R.	OTHER ACCOUNTS CREDIT	ACCOUNTS RECEIVABLE CREDIT	SALES CREDIT	SALES DISCOUNTS DEBIT	CASH DEBIT
Dec.	2	Wilson Wilde	Invoice 11/23	✓		4200 00		84 00	4116 00
	15	Sales	Cash sales	✓			3883 00		3883 00
	15	Marge Craig	Invoice 12/6	✓		2450 00		49 00	2401 00

CASH DISBURSEMENTS JOURNAL

Page 4

DATE		CH. NO.	PAYEE	ACCOUNT DEBITED	P.R.	OTHER ACCOUNTS DEBIT	ACCOUNTS PAYABLE DEBIT	PURCHASES DISCOUNTS CREDIT	CASH CREDIT
Dec.	2	619	Omni Realty Co.	Rent Expense	640	2250 00			2250 00
	6	620	Fireside Company	Fireside Company	✓		3800 00	76 00	3724 00
	12	621	Weathers Company	Weathers Company	✓		3200 00	64 00	3136 00
	15	622	Jamie Forster	Sales Salaries Expense	621	1620 00			1620 00

GENERAL JOURNAL

Page 2

DATE	ACCOUNT TITLES AND EXPLANATION	P.R.	DEBIT	CREDIT
Dec. 4	Accounts Payable—Fireside Company	201/✓	4 6 0 00	
	Purchases Returns and Allowances	506		4 6 0 00
9	Sales Returns and Allowances	414	8 5 0 00	
	Accounts Receivable—Marge Craig	106/✓		8 5 0 00

ACCOUNTS RECEIVABLE LEDGER

NAME   Marge Craig

ADDRESS   5118 Meadow Creek Dr.

DATE	EXPLANATION	P.R.	DEBIT	CREDIT	BALANCE
Dec. 6		S3	3 3 0 0 00		3 3 0 0 00
9		G2		8 5 0 00	2 4 5 0 00
15		R3		2 4 5 0 00	- 0 -

NAME   Ambrose Fielder

ADDRESS   7006 Windridge Cove

DATE	EXPLANATION	P.R.	DEBIT	CREDIT	BALANCE
Dec. 12		S3	3 6 5 0 00		3 6 5 0 00

NAME   Amy Oakley

ADDRESS   2406 Rio Grande St.

DATE	EXPLANATION	P.R.	DEBIT	CREDIT	BALANCE
Dec. 15		S3	3 1 0 0 00		3 1 0 0 00

NAME   Wilson Wilde

ADDRESS   823 West 15th St.

DATE	EXPLANATION	P.R.	DEBIT	CREDIT	BALANCE
Nov. 23		S2	4 2 0 0 00		4 2 0 0 00
Dec. 2		R3		4 2 0 0 00	- 0 -

ACCOUNTS PAYABLE LEDGER

NAME   Fireside Company

ADDRESS   7812 Beauregard Circle

DATE	EXPLANATION	P.R.	DEBIT	CREDIT	BALANCE
Nov. 28		P1		4 2 6 0 00	4 2 6 0 00
Dec. 4		G2	4 6 0 00		3 8 0 0 00
6		D4	3 8 0 0 00		- 0 -

NAME   Gray Supply Company

ADDRESS   10300 Springdale Rd.

DATE	EXPLANATION	P.R.	DEBIT	CREDIT	BALANCE
Dec. 5		P2		1 3 0 0 00	1 3 0 0 00

NAME   Sunshine Company

ADDRESS   2103 Redwing Way

DATE	EXPLANATION	P.R.	DEBIT	CREDIT	BALANCE
Dec. 15		P2		2 6 5 0 00	2 6 5 0 00

NAME   Weathers Company
ADDRESS   630 Shadow Mountain Dr.

DATE	EXPLANATION	P.R.	DEBIT	CREDIT	BALANCE
Dec. 2		P2		3 2 0 0 00	3 2 0 0 00
12		D4	3 2 0 0 00		- 0 -
15		P2		3 9 9 0 00	3 9 9 0 00

GENERAL LEDGER

Cash   Account No. 101

DATE	EXPLANATION	P.R.	DEBIT	CREDIT	BALANCE
Nov. 30	Balance	✓			5 3 6 1 00

Accounts Receivable   Account No. 106

DATE	EXPLANATION	P.R.	DEBIT	CREDIT	BALANCE
Nov. 30	Balance	✓			4 2 0 0 00
Dec. 9		G2		8 5 0 00	3 3 5 0 00

Merchandise Inventory   Account No. 119

DATE	EXPLANATION	P.R.	DEBIT	CREDIT	BALANCE
Nov. 30	Balance	✓			66 9 7 0 00

Office Supplies   Account No. 124

DATE	EXPLANATION	P.R.	DEBIT	CREDIT	BALANCE
Nov. 30	Balance	✓			6 0 7 00

Store Supplies   Account No. 125

DATE	EXPLANATION	P.R.	DEBIT	CREDIT	BALANCE
Nov. 30	Balance	✓			3 4 6 00

Store Equipment   Account No. 165

DATE	EXPLANATION	P.R.	DEBIT	CREDIT	BALANCE
Nov. 30	Balance	✓			42 1 2 9 00

Accumulated Depreciation, Store Equipment   Account No. 166

DATE	EXPLANATION	P.R.	DEBIT	CREDIT	BALANCE
Nov. 30	Balance	✓			9 1 5 3 00

Accounts Payable   Account No. 201

DATE	EXPLANATION	P.R.	DEBIT	CREDIT	BALANCE
Nov. 30	Balance	✓			4 2 6 0 00
Dec. 4		G2	4 6 0 00		3 8 0 0 00

Marlin Levy, Capital   Account No. 301

DATE	EXPLANATION	P.R.	DEBIT	CREDIT	BALANCE
Nov. 30	Balance	✓			106 2 0 0 00

Marlin Levy, Withdrawals   Account No. 302

DATE	EXPLANATION	P.R.	DEBIT	CREDIT	BALANCE

Sales   Account No. 413

DATE	EXPLANATION	P.R.	DEBIT	CREDIT	BALANCE

Sales Returns and Allowances   Account No. 414

DATE	EXPLANATION	P.R.	DEBIT	CREDIT	BALANCE
Dec. 9		G2	850 00		850 00

Sales Discounts   Account No. 415

DATE	EXPLANATION	P.R.	DEBIT	CREDIT	BALANCE

Purchases   Account No. 505

DATE	EXPLANATION	P.R.	DEBIT	CREDIT	BALANCE

Purchases Returns and Allowances   Account No. 506

DATE	EXPLANATION	P.R.	DEBIT	CREDIT	BALANCE
Dec. 4		G2		460 00	460 00

Purchases Discounts   Account No. 507

DATE	EXPLANATION	P.R.	DEBIT	CREDIT	BALANCE

Sales Salaries Expense   Account No. 621

DATE	EXPLANATION	P.R.	DEBIT	CREDIT	BALANCE
Dec. 15		D4	1 620 00		1 620 00

Rent Expense   Account No. 640

DATE	EXPLANATION	P.R.	DEBIT	CREDIT	BALANCE
Dec. 2		D4	2 250 00		2 250 00

Utilities Expense   Account No. 690

DATE	EXPLANATION	P.R.	DEBIT	CREDIT	BALANCE

Purchases Returns and Allowances   Account No. 506

DATE	EXPLANATION	P.R.	DEBIT	CREDIT	BALANCE

Purchases Discounts   Account No. 507

DATE	EXPLANATION	P.R.	DEBIT	CREDIT	BALANCE

Sales Salaries Expense   Account No. 621

DATE	EXPLANATION	P.R.	DEBIT	CREDIT	BALANCE

ACCOUNTS RECEIVABLE LEDGER

NAME   Marjorie Cobb

ADDRESS   4314 East Oak Avenue

DATE	EXPLANATION	P.R.	DEBIT	CREDIT	BALANCE

NAME   Leroy Hazzard

ADDRESS   1412 West 24th Street

DATE	EXPLANATION	P.R.	DEBIT	CREDIT	BALANCE

NAME   Sam Segura

ADDRESS   3434 West 18th Street

DATE	EXPLANATION	P.R.	DEBIT	CREDIT	BALANCE

ACCOUNTS PAYABLE LEDGER

NAME   Arnot Company

ADDRESS   1212 Ninth Avenue

DATE	EXPLANATION	P.R.	DEBIT	CREDIT	BALANCE

NAME   Defore Industries

ADDRESS   15th and Oak

DATE	EXPLANATION	P.R.	DEBIT	CREDIT	BALANCE

NAME   Jett Supply

ADDRESS   32nd and Maple

DATE	EXPLANATION	P.R.	DEBIT	CREDIT	BALANCE

NAME   The Welch Company

ADDRESS   1412 East Maple Avenue

DATE	EXPLANATION	P.R.	DEBIT	CREDIT	BALANCE

SALES JOURNAL

DATE	ACCOUNT DEBITED	INVOICE NUMBER	P.R.	AMOUNT

CASH RECEIPTS JOURNAL

DATE	ACCOUNT CREDITED	EXPLANATION	P.R.	OTHER ACCOUNTS CREDIT	ACCOUNTS RECEIVABLE CREDIT	SALES CREDIT	SALES DISCOUNTS DEBIT	CASH DEBIT

GENERAL LEDGER

Cash   Account No. 111

DATE	EXPLANATION	P.R.	DEBIT	CREDIT	BALANCE

Accounts Receivable   Account No. 112

DATE	EXPLANATION	P.R.	DEBIT	CREDIT	BALANCE

Notes Payable   Account No. 211

DATE	EXPLANATION	P.R.	DEBIT	CREDIT	BALANCE

Sales   Account No. 411

DATE	EXPLANATION	P.R.	DEBIT	CREDIT	BALANCE

Sales Discounts   Account No. 413

DATE	EXPLANATION	P.R.	DEBIT	CREDIT	BALANCE

ACCOUNTS RECEIVABLE LEDGER

Regina Niser

DATE	EXPLANATION	P.R.	DEBIT	CREDIT	BALANCE

Helen Stone

DATE	EXPLANATION	P.R.	DEBIT	CREDIT	BALANCE

PURCHASES JOURNAL

DATE	ACCOUNT	DATE OF INVOICE	TERMS	P.R.	ACCOUNTS PAYABLE CREDIT	PURCHASES DEBIT	OTHER ACCOUNTS DEBIT

CASH DISBURSEMENTS JOURNAL

DATE	CH. NO.	PAYEE	ACCOUNT DEBITED	P.R.	OTHER ACCOUNTS DEBIT	ACCOUNTS PAYABLE DEBIT	PURCHASES DISCOUNTS CREDIT	CASH CREDIT

GENERAL JOURNAL

DATE	ACCOUNT TITLES AND EXPLANATION	P.R.	DEBIT	CREDIT

GENERAL LEDGER

Cash   Account No. 101

DATE	EXPLANATION	P.R.	DEBIT	CREDIT	BALANCE

Store Supplies   Account No. 125

DATE	EXPLANATION	P.R.	DEBIT	CREDIT	BALANCE

Store Equipment   Account No. 165

DATE	EXPLANATION	P.R.	DEBIT	CREDIT	BALANCE

Accounts Payable   Account No. 201

DATE	EXPLANATION	P.R.	DEBIT	CREDIT	BALANCE

Notes Payable   Account No. 251

DATE	EXPLANATION	P.R.	DEBIT	CREDIT	BALANCE

Purchases   Account No. 505

DATE	EXPLANATION	P.R.	DEBIT	CREDIT	BALANCE

Purchases Returns and Allowances   Account No. 506

DATE	EXPLANATION	P.R.	DEBIT	CREDIT	BALANCE

Purchases Discounts   Account No. 507

DATE	EXPLANATION	P.R.	DEBIT	CREDIT	BALANCE

Sales Salaries Expense   Account No. 621

DATE	EXPLANATION	P.R.	DEBIT	CREDIT	BALANCE

	Advertising Expense					Account No. 655
DATE	EXPLANATION	P.R.	DEBIT	CREDIT	BALANCE	

ACCOUNTS PAYABLE LEDGER

Barclay Company

DATE	EXPLANATION	P.R.	DEBIT	CREDIT	BALANCE

Long Company

DATE	EXPLANATION	P.R.	DEBIT	CREDIT	BALANCE

Nixen Company

DATE	EXPLANATION	P.R.	DEBIT	CREDIT	BALANCE

Rexor Company

DATE	EXPLANATION	P.R.	DEBIT	CREDIT	BALANCE

Page 3

SALES JOURNAL

DATE		ACCOUNT DEBITED	INVOICE NUMBER	P.R.	AMOUNT
Jan	6	Fred Midler	738	√	3 6 4 5 00
	15	Brenda Simms	739	√	4 0 5 0 00
	18	Sam Trent	740	√	3 4 4 5 00

Page 2

PURCHASES JOURNAL

DATE		ACCOUNT	DATE OF INVOICE	TERMS	P.R.	ACCOUNTS PAYABLE CREDIT	PURCHASES DEBIT	STORE SUPPLIES DEBIT	OFFICE SUPPLIES DEIBT
Jan.	2	Younger Company	Jan. 2	2/10,n/60		3 6 0 0 00	3 6 0 0 00		
	5	Reed Suppliers	Jan. 3	n/10 EOM		1 6 4 5 00	1 3 5 0 00	2 2 0 00	7 5 00
	17	Younger Company	Jan. 15	2/10, n/60		4 4 3 5 00	4 4 3 5 00		
	18	Vax Company	Jan. 16	2/10, n/60		2 9 5 0 00	2 9 5 0 00		

CASH RECEIPTS JOURNAL

Page 3

DATE		ACCOUNT CREDITED	EXPLANATION	P.R.	OTHER ACCOUNTS CREDIT	ACCOUNTS RECEIVABLE CREDIT	SALES CREDIT	SALES DISCOUNTS DEBIT	CASH DEBIT
Jan	2	Maria Perez	Invoice Dec. 23	√		4750 00		95 00	4655 00
	15	Sales	Cash sales	√			43155 00		43155 00
	16	Fred Bidler	Invoice Jan. 6	√		2700 00		54 00	2646 00

CASH DISBURSEMENTS JOURNAL

Page 4

DATE		CH. NO.	PAYEE	ACCOUNT DEBITED	P.R.	OTHER ACCOUNTS DEBIT	ACCOUNTS PAYABLE DEBIT	PURCHASES DISCOUNTS CREDIT	CASH CREDIT
Jan.	2	446	Property Management Co.	Rent Expense	640	2500 00			3500 00
	6	447	Eclat Company	Eclat Company	√		4250 00	85 00	4165 00
	12	448	Younger Company	Younger Company	√		3600 00	72 00	3528 00
	15	449	Max Davus	Sales Salaries Expense	621	1440 00			1440 00

GENERAL JOURNAL

DATE	ACCOUNT TITLES AND EXPLANATION	P.R.	DEBIT	CREDIT
Jan. 4	Accounts Payable—Eclat Company	201/√	5 1 5 00	
	Purchases Returns and Allowances	506		5 1 5 00
9	Sales Returns and Allowances	414	9 4 5 00	
	Accounts Receivable—Fred Bidler	106/√		9 4 5 00

ACCOUNTS RECEIVABLE LEDGER

Fred Midler

DATE	EXPLANATION	P.R.	DEBIT	CREDIT	BALANCE
Jan. 6		S3	3 6 4 5 00		3 6 4 5 00
9		G2		9 4 5 00	2 7 0 0 00
16		R3		2 7 0 0 00	- 0 -

Brenda Simms

DATE	EXPLANATION	P.R.	DEBIT	CREDIT	BALANCE
Jan. 15		S3	4 0 5 0 00		4 0 5 0 00

Sam Trent

DATE	EXPLANATION	P.R.	DEBIT	CREDIT	BALANCE
Jan. 18		S3	3 4 4 5 00		3 4 4 5 00

Frank Urich

DATE	EXPLANATION	P.R.	DEBIT	CREDIT	BALANCE
Dec. 23		S2	4 7 5 0 00		4 7 5 0 00
Jan. 2		R3		4 7 5 0 00	- 0 -

ACCOUNTS PAYABLE LEDGER

Eclat Company

DATE	EXPLANATION	P.R.	DEBIT	CREDIT	BALANCE
Dec. 28		P1		4 7 6 5 00	4 7 6 5 00
Jan. 4		G@	5 1 5 00		4 2 5 0 00
6		D4	4 2 5 0 00		- 0 -

Reed Suppliers

DATE	EXPLANATION	P.R.	DEBIT	CREDIT	BALANCE
Jan. 5		P2		1 6 4 5 00	1 6 4 5 00

Vax Company

DATE	EXPLANATION	P.R.	DEBIT	CREDIT	BALANCE
Jan. 18		P2		2 9 5 0 00	2 9 5 0 00

Younger Company

DATE	EXPLANATION	P.R.	DEBIT	CREDIT	BALANCE
Jan. 2		P2		3 6 0 0 00	3 6 0 0 00
12		D4	3 6 0 0 00		- 0 -
17		D4		4 4 3 5 00	4 4 3 5 00

GENERAL LEDGER

Cash   Account No. 101

DATE	EXPLANATION	P.R.	DEBIT	CREDIT	BALANCE
Dec. 31	Balance	√			5 8 9 5 00

Accounts Receivable   Account No. 106

DATE	EXPLANATION	P.R.	DEBIT	CREDIT	BALANCE
Dec. 31	Balance	√			4 7 5 0 00
Jan. 9		G2		9 4 5 00	3 8 0 5 00

Merchandise Inventory   Account No. 119

DATE	EXPLANATION	P.R.	DEBIT	CREDIT	BALANCE
Dec. 31	Balance	√			74 4 2 0 00

Office Supplies   Account No. 124

DATE	EXPLANATION	P.R.	DEBIT	CREDIT	BALANCE
Dec. 31	Balance	√			3 8 5 00

Store Supplies   Account No. 125

DATE	EXPLANATION	P.R.	DEBIT	CREDIT	BALANCE
Dec. 31	Balance	√			6 7 5 00

Store Equipment   Account No. 165

DATE	EXPLANATION	P.R.	DEBIT	CREDIT	BALANCE
Dec. 31	Balance	√			46 8 1 0 00

Accumulated Amortization, Store Equipment   Account No. 166

DATE	EXPLANATION	P.R.	DEBIT	CREDIT	BALANCE
Dec. 31	Balance	√			10 1 7 0 00

Accounts Payable   Account No. 201

DATE	EXPLANATION	P.R.	DEBIT	CREDIT	BALANCE
Dec. 31	Balance	√			4 7 6 5 00
Jan. 4		G2	5 1 5 00		4 2 5 0 00

Susan Linder, Capital   Account No. 301

DATE	EXPLANATION	P.R.	DEBIT	CREDIT	BALANCE
Dec. 31	Balance	√			118 0 0 0 00

Susan Linder, Withdrawals   Account No. 302

DATE	EXPLANATION	P.R.	DEBIT	CREDIT	BALANCE

Sales   Account No. 413

DATE	EXPLANATION	P.R.	DEBIT	CREDIT	BALANCE

Sales Returns and Allowances   Account No. 414

DATE	EXPLANATION	P.R.	DEBIT	CREDIT	BALANCE
Jan. 9		G2	945 00		945 00

Sales Discounts   Account No. 415

DATE	EXPLANATION	P.R.	DEBIT	CREDIT	BALANCE

Purchases   Account No. 505

DATE	EXPLANATION	P.R.	DEBIT	CREDIT	BALANCE

Purchases Returns and Allowances   Account No. 506

DATE	EXPLANATION	P.R.	DEBIT	CREDIT	BALANCE
Jan. 4		G2		515 00	515 00

Purchases Discounts   Account No. 507

DATE	EXPLANATION	P.R.	DEBIT	CREDIT	BALANCE

Sales Salaries Expense   Account No. 621

DATE	EXPLANATION	P.R.	DEBIT	CREDIT	BALANCE
Jan. 15		D4	1 440 00		1 440 00

	Rent Expense				Account No. 640	
DATE	EXPLANATION	P.R.	DEBIT	CREDIT	BALANCE	
Jan. 2		D4	2 5 0 0 00		2 5 0 0 00	

	Utilities Expense				Account No. 690	
DATE	EXPLANATION	P.R.	DEBIT	CREDIT	BALANCE	

SALES JOURNAL

DATE	ACCOUNT DEBITED	INVOICE NUMBER	P.R.	SALES CREDIT	GST CREDIT	PST CREDIT	ACCOUNTS RECEIVABLE DEBIT

PURCHASES JOURNAL

DATE	ACCOUNT	DATE OF INVOICE	TERMS	P.R.	ACCOUNTS PAYABLE CREDIT	PURCHASES DEBIT	STORE SUPPLIES DEBIT	OFFICE SUPPLIES DEBIT

Page 2

CASH RECEIPTS JOURNAL

DATE	ACCOUNT CREDITED	EXPLANATION	P.R.	OTHER ACCOUNTS CREDIT	SALES CREDIT	GST CREDIT	PST DEBIT	ACCOUNTS RECEIVABLE CREDIT	DISCOUNT DEBIT	CASH DEBIT

Page 4

CASH DISBURSEMENTS JOURNAL

DATE	CH. NO.	PAYEE	ACCOUNT DEBITED	P.R.	OTHER ACCOUNTS DEBIT	ACCOUNTS PAYABLE DEBIT	PURCHASES DISCOUNTS CREDIT	CASH CREDIT

GENERAL JOURNAL

DATE	ACCOUNT TITLES AND EXPLANATION	P.R.	DEBIT	CREDIT

GENERAL LEDGER

Cash   Account No. 101

DATE	EXPLANATION	P.R.	DEBIT	CREDIT	BALANCE

Accounts Receivable   Account No. 106

DATE	EXPLANATION	P.R.	DEBIT	CREDIT	BALANCE

Office Supplies   Account No. 124

DATE	EXPLANATION	P.R.	DEBIT	CREDIT	BALANCE

Store Supplies   Account No. 125

DATE	EXPLANATION	P.R.	DEBIT	CREDIT	BALANCE

Office Equipment   Account No. 163

DATE	EXPLANATION	P.R.	DEBIT	CREDIT	BALANCE

Accounts Payable   Account No. 201

DATE	EXPLANATION	P.R.	DEBIT	CREDIT	BALANCE

PST Payable   Account No. 224

DATE	EXPLANATION	P.R.	DEBIT	CREDIT	BALANCE

GST Payable   Account No. 225

DATE	EXPLANATION	P.R.	DEBIT	CREDIT	BALANCE

Notes Payable   Account No. 251

DATE	EXPLANATION	P.R.	DEBIT	CREDIT	BALANCE

Sales   Account No. 413

DATE	EXPLANATION	P.R.	DEBIT	CREDIT	BALANCE

Sales Discounts   Account No. 415

DATE	EXPLANATION	P.R.	DEBIT	CREDIT	BALANCE

Purchases   Account No. 505

DATE	EXPLANATION	P.R.	DEBIT	CREDIT	BALANCE

Purchases Returns and Allowances   Account No. 506

DATE	EXPLANATION	P.R.	DEBIT	CREDIT	BALANCE

Purchases Discounts   Account No. 507

DATE	EXPLANATION	P.R.	DEBIT	CREDIT	BALANCE

Sales Salaries Expense   Account No. 621

DATE	EXPLANATION	P.R.	DEBIT	CREDIT	BALANCE

ACCOUNTS RECEIVABLE LEDGER

Carl Chase

DATE	EXPLANATION	P.R.	DEBIT	CREDIT	BALANCE

Omar Hanes

DATE	EXPLANATION	P.R.	DEBIT	CREDIT	BALANCE

Leigh Rogers

DATE	EXPLANATION	P.R.	DEBIT	CREDIT	BALANCE

ACCOUNTS PAYABLE LEDGER

Abell Company

DATE	EXPLANATION	P.R.	DEBIT	CREDIT	BALANCE

Bradley Company

DATE	EXPLANATION	P.R.	DEBIT	CREDIT	BALANCE

Telecore Company

DATE	EXPLANATION	P.R.	DEBIT	CREDIT	BALANCE

Thomas Company

DATE	EXPLANATION	P.R.	DEBIT	CREDIT	BALANCE

SALES JOURNAL — Page 2

DATE	ACCOUNT DEBITED	INVOICE NUMBER	P.R.	AMOUNT

PURCHASES JOURNAL — Page 2

DATE	ACCOUNT	DATE OF INVOICE	TERMS	P.R.	PURCHASES DEBIT	OFFICE SUPPLIES DEBIT	OTHER ACCOUNTS DEBIT	ACCOUNTS PAYABLE CREDIT

Page 2

CASH RECEIPTS JOURNAL

DATE	ACCOUNT CREDITED	EXPLANATION	P.R.	OTHER ACCOUNTS CREDIT	ACCOUNTS RECEIVABLE CREDIT	SALES CREDIT	SALES DISCOUNTS DEBIT	CASH DEBIT

Page 2

CASH DISBURSEMENTS JOURNAL

DATE	CH. NO.	PAYEE	ACCOUNT DEBITED	P.R.	OTHER ACCOUNTS DEBIT	ACCOUNTS PAYABLE DEBIT	PURCHASES DISCOUNTS CREDIT	CASH CREDIT

GENERAL JOURNAL

DATE	ACCOUNT TITLES AND EXPLANATION	P.R.	DEBIT	CREDIT

DATE	ACCOUNT TITLES AND EXPLANATION	P.R.	DEBIT	CREDIT

GENERAL LEDGER

Cash   Account No. 101

DATE	EXPLANATION	P.R.	DEBIT	CREDIT	BALANCE
19— Jul. 31	Balance	✓			35 8 9 1 00

Accounts Receivable   Account No. 106

DATE	EXPLANATION	P.R.	DEBIT	CREDIT	BALANCE
19— Jul. 31	Balance	✓			3 3 7 5 00

Merchandise Inventory   Account No. 119

DATE	EXPLANATION	P.R.	DEBIT	CREDIT	BALANCE
19— Jul. 31	Balance	✓			157 2 0 0 00

Office Supplies   Account No. 124

DATE	EXPLANATION	P.R.	DEBIT	CREDIT	BALANCE
19— Jul. 31	Balance	✓			3 0 7 00

Store Supplies   Account No. 125

DATE	EXPLANATION	P.R.	DEBIT	CREDIT	BALANCE
19— Jul. 31	Balance	✓			1 7 4 8 00

COMPREHENSIVE PROBLEM
Regis Company (Continued)

Prepaid Insurance   Account No. 128

DATE	EXPLANATION	P.R.	DEBIT	CREDIT	BALANCE
19— Jul. 31	Balance	✓			2 3 7 0 00

Office Equipment   Account No. 163

DATE	EXPLANATION	P.R.	DEBIT	CREDIT	BALANCE
19— Jul. 31	Balance	✓			16 0 5 0 00

Accumulated Depreciation, Office Equipment   Account No. 164

DATE	EXPLANATION	P.R.	DEBIT	CREDIT	BALANCE
19— Jul. 31	Balance	✓			7 0 7 0 00

Store Equipment   Account No. 165

DATE	EXPLANATION	P.R.	DEBIT	CREDIT	BALANCE
19— Jul. 31	Balance	✓			27 8 0 0 00

Accumulated Depreciation, Store Equipment   Account No. 166

DATE	EXPLANATION	P.R.	DEBIT	CREDIT	BALANCE
19— Jul. 31	Balance	✓			12 5 4 0 00

Accounts Payable   Account No. 201

DATE	EXPLANATION	P.R.	DEBIT	CREDIT	BALANCE
19— Jul. 31	Balance	✓			5 0 7 0 00

Walt Regis, Capital   Account No. 301

DATE	EXPLANATION	P.R.	DEBIT	CREDIT	BALANCE
19— Jul. 31	Balance	✓			220 0 6 1 00

Walt Regis, Withdrawals   Account No. 302

DATE	EXPLANATION	P.R.	DEBIT	CREDIT	BALANCE

Sales   Account No. 413

DATE	EXPLANATION	P.R.	DEBIT	CREDIT	BALANCE

Sales Returns and Allowances   Account No. 414

DATE	EXPLANATION	P.R.	DEBIT	CREDIT	BALANCE

Sales Discounts — Account No. 415

DATE	EXPLANATION	P.R.	DEBIT	CREDIT	BALANCE

Purchases — Account No. 505

DATE	EXPLANATION	P.R.	DEBIT	CREDIT	BALANCE

Purchases Returns and Allowances — Account No. 506

DATE	EXPLANATION	P.R.	DEBIT	CREDIT	BALANCE

Purchases Discounts — Account No. 507

DATE	EXPLANATION	P.R.	DEBIT	CREDIT	BALANCE

Depreciation Expense, Office Equipment — Account No. 612

DATE	EXPLANATION	P.R.	DEBIT	CREDIT	BALANCE

Depreciation Expense, Store Equipment — Account No. 613

DATE	EXPLANATION	P.R.	DEBIT	CREDIT	BALANCE

Office Salaries Expense — Account No. 620

DATE	EXPLANATION	P.R.	DEBIT	CREDIT	BALANCE

Sales Salaries Expense — Account No. 621

DATE	EXPLANATION	P.R.	DEBIT	CREDIT	BALANCE

Insurance Expense — Account No. 637

DATE	EXPLANATION	P.R.	DEBIT	CREDIT	BALANCE

Rent Expense, Office Space — Account No. 641

DATE	EXPLANATION	P.R.	DEBIT	CREDIT	BALANCE

Rent Expense, Selling Space — Account No. 642

DATE	EXPLANATION	P.R.	DEBIT	CREDIT	BALANCE

Office Supplies Expense — Account No. 650

DATE	EXPLANATION	P.R.	DEBIT	CREDIT	BALANCE

Store Supplies Expense — Account No. 651

DATE	EXPLANATION	P.R.	DEBIT	CREDIT	BALANCE

Utilities Expense — Account No. 690

DATE	EXPLANATION	P.R.	DEBIT	CREDIT	BALANCE

Income Summary — Account No. 901

DATE	EXPLANATION	P.R.	DEBIT	CREDIT	BALANCE

ACCOUNTS RECEIVABLE LEDGER

NAME   Anchor Services
ADDRESS   1212 North Bay

DATE	EXPLANATION	P.R.	DEBIT	CREDIT	BALANCE

NAME   Franzetti Company
ADDRESS   2000 Industry Road

DATE	EXPLANATION	P.R.	DEBIT	CREDIT	BALANCE

NAME   L&M Company

ADDRESS   407 North 15th Street

DATE	EXPLANATION	P.R.	DEBIT	CREDIT	BALANCE

NAME   Prime, Inc.

ADDRESS   124 Washington Avenue

DATE	EXPLANATION	P.R.	DEBIT	CREDIT	BALANCE
19— July 28		S2	3 3 7 5 00		3 3 7 5 00

ACCOUNTS PAYABLE LEDGER

NAME   Discount Supplies

ADDRESS   7300 Falcon Ledge

DATE	EXPLANATION	P.R.	DEBIT	CREDIT	BALANCE

NAME   Mayfair Corp.

ADDRESS   13 Oakdale

DATE	EXPLANATION	P.R.	DEBIT	CREDIT	BALANCE

COMPREHENSIVE PROBLEM
Regis Company (Continued)

NAME   Signature Products

ADDRESS 1212 Castle Ridge

DATE	EXPLANATION	P.R.	DEBIT	CREDIT	BALANCE
19— July 29		P2	5 0 7 0 00		5 0 7 0 00

NAME   Tranh Industries

ADDRESS 725 St. Johns Boulevard

DATE	EXPLANATION	P.R.	DEBIT	CREDIT	BALANCE

REGIS COMPANY
Work Sheet
For Year Ended August 31, 19—

ACCOUNT TITLES	TRIAL BALANCE		ADJUSTMENTS		INCOME STATEMENT		STATEMENT OF CHANGES IN OWNER'S EQUITY AND BALANCE SHEET	
	DR.	CR.	DR.	CR.	DR.	CR.	DR.	CR.

COMPREHENSIVE PROBLEM
Regis Company (Continued)

REGIS COMPANY

Income Statement

For Month Ended August 31, 19—

REGIS COMPANY

Statement of Changes in Owner's Equity

For Month Ended August 31, 19—

REGIS COMPANY

Balance Sheet

August 31, 19—

REGIS COMPANY

Post-Closing Trial Balance

August 31, 19—

REGIS COMPANY

Schedule of Accounts Receivable

August 31, 19—

REGIS COMPANY

Schedule of Accounts Payable

August 31, 19—

Name _____

EXERCISE 7–2

EXERCISE 7-4

Page 1

DATE	ACCOUNT TITLES AND EXPLANATION	P.R.	DEBIT	CREDIT

GENERAL JOURNAL

DATE	ACCOUNT TITLES AND EXPLANATION	P.R.	DEBIT	CREDIT

EXERCISE 7–6

GENERAL JOURNAL

DATE	ACCOUNT TITLES AND EXPLANATION	P.R.	DEBIT	CREDIT

EXERCISE 7–8

GENERAL JOURNAL

DATE	ACCOUNT TITLES AND EXPLANATION	P.R.	DEBIT	CREDIT

Part 1

GENERAL JOURNAL

Page 1

DATE	ACCOUNT TITLES AND EXPLANATION	P.R.	DEBIT	CREDIT

Part 2

			DEBIT	CREDIT

GENERAL JOURNAL   Page 2

DATE	ACCOUNT TITLES AND EXPLANATION	P.R.	DEBIT	CREDIT

Part 4

Name _____

GENERAL JOURNAL

Page 1

DATE	ACCOUNT TITLES AND EXPLANATION	P.R.	DEBIT	CREDIT

GENERAL JOURNAL   Page 1

DATE	ACCOUNT TITLES AND EXPLANATION	P.R.	DEBIT	CREDIT

Part 3

Part 1

GENERAL JOURNAL

Page 1

DATE	ACCOUNT TITLES AND EXPLANATION	P.R.	DEBIT	CREDIT

Part 2

GENERAL JOURNAL

Page 1

DATE	ACCOUNT TITLES AND EXPLANATION	P.R.	DEBIT	CREDIT

GENERAL JOURNAL   Page 1

DATE	ACCOUNT TITLES AND EXPLANATION	P.R.	DEBIT	CREDIT
Part 1				
Part 2				

GENERAL JOURNAL   Page 1

DATE	ACCOUNT TITLES AND EXPLANATION	P.R.	DEBIT	CREDIT
Part 1				

Part 2

DATE	ACCOUNT TITLES AND EXPLANATION	P.R.	DEBIT	CREDIT

GENERAL JOURNAL

DATE	ACCOUNT TITLES AND EXPLANATION	P.R.	DEBIT	CREDIT
Part 3				

GENERAL JOURNAL   Page 1

DATE	ACCOUNT TITLES AND EXPLANATION	P.R.	DEBIT	CREDIT

Part 2

GENERAL JOURNAL   Page 1

DATE	ACCOUNT TITLES AND EXPLANATION	P.R.	DEBIT	CREDIT

GENERAL JOURNAL   Page 1

DATE	ACCOUNT TITLES AND EXPLANATION	P.R.	DEBIT	CREDIT

EXERCISE 8–3

GENERAL JOURNAL   Page 1

DATE	ACCOUNT TITLES AND EXPLANATION	P.R.	DEBIT	CREDIT

EXERCISE 8–4

GENERAL JOURNAL   Page 1

DATE	ACCOUNT TITLES AND EXPLANATION	P.R.	DEBIT	CREDIT

Name _____

GENERAL LEDGER

Accounts Receivable	Sales	Sales Returns and Allowances

ACCOUNTS RECEIVABLE LEDGER

Barbara Fowler	Robert Guerrero	Chris Layton

GENERAL JOURNAL

Page 1

DATE	ACCOUNT TITLES AND EXPLANATION	P.R.	DEBIT	CREDIT

EXERCISE 8–7

GENERAL JOURNAL

Page 1

DATE	ACCOUNT TITLES AND EXPLANATION	P.R.	DEBIT	CREDIT

EXERCISE 8–8

GENERAL JOURNAL

Page 1

DATE	ACCOUNT TITLES AND EXPLANATION	P.R.	DEBIT	CREDIT

GENERAL JOURNAL

DATE	ACCOUNT TITLES AND EXPLANATION	P.R.	DEBIT	CREDIT

GENERAL JOURNAL

DATE	ACCOUNT TITLES AND EXPLANATION	P.R.	DEBIT	CREDIT

DATE	ACCOUNT TITLES AND EXPLANATION	P.R.	DEBIT	CREDIT

Part 3

GENERAL JOURNAL   Page 3

DATE	ACCOUNT TITLES AND EXPLANATION	P.R.	DEBIT	CREDIT

Name _____

GENERAL JOURNAL

DATE	ACCOUNT TITLES AND EXPLANATION	P.R.	DEBIT	CREDIT

DATE	ACCOUNT TITLES AND EXPLANATION	P.R.	DEBIT	CREDIT

Part 1

GENERAL JOURNAL   Page 1

DATE	ACCOUNT TITLES AND EXPLANATION	P.R.	DEBIT	CREDIT

Part 3

_____
_____
_____
_____
_____
_____
_____
_____
_____
_____
_____
_____
_____
_____
_____
_____
_____
_____
_____

Part 2

GENERAL JOURNAL

Page 1

DATE	ACCOUNT TITLES AND EXPLANATION	P.R.	DEBIT	CREDIT

Name _____

GENERAL JOURNAL

DATE	ACCOUNT TITLES AND EXPLANATION	P.R.	DEBIT	CREDIT

DATE	ACCOUNT TITLES AND EXPLANATION	P.R.	DEBIT	CREDIT

Name _____

GENERAL JOURNAL

DATE	ACCOUNT TITLES AND EXPLANATION	P.R.	DEBIT	CREDIT

DATE	ACCOUNT TITLES AND EXPLANATION	P.R.	DEBIT	CREDIT

Name _____

GENERAL JOURNAL

DATE	ACCOUNT TITLES AND EXPLANATION	P.R.	DEBIT	CREDIT

DATE	ACCOUNT TITLES AND EXPLANATION	P.R.	DEBIT	CREDIT

Name _____

GENERAL JOURNAL

DATE	ACCOUNT TITLES AND EXPLANATION	P.R.	DEBIT	CREDIT

DATE	ACCOUNT TITLES AND EXPLANATION	P.R.	DEBIT	CREDIT

DATE	ACCOUNT TITLES AND EXPLANATION	P.R.	DEBIT	CREDIT

Part 3

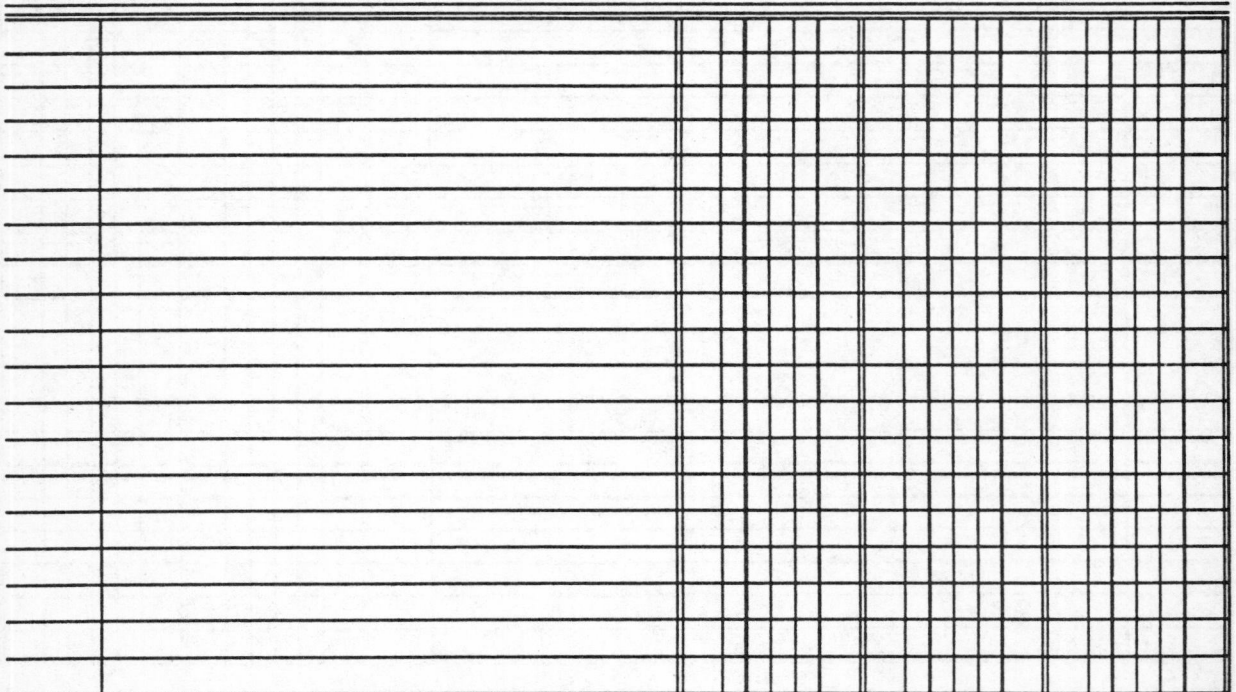

Part 1

Part 2

GENERAL JOURNAL   Page 1

DATE	ACCOUNT TITLES AND EXPLANATION	P.R.	DEBIT	CREDIT

GENERAL JOURNAL

DATE	ACCOUNT TITLES AND EXPLANATION	P.R.	DEBIT	CREDIT

Name _____

GENERAL JOURNAL

DATE	ACCOUNT TITLES AND EXPLANATION	P.R.	DEBIT	CREDIT

Page 2

DATE	ACCOUNT TITLES AND EXPLANATION	P.R.	DEBIT	CREDIT
Part 1				
Part 2				
Part 3				

_____
_____
_____
_____
_____
_____
_____
_____
_____
_____
_____
_____
_____

Part 2

GENERAL JOURNAL   Page 1

DATE	ACCOUNT TITLES AND EXPLANATION	P.R.	DEBIT	CREDIT

GENERAL JOURNAL

DATE	ACCOUNT TITLES AND EXPLANATION	P.R.	DEBIT	CREDIT

DATE	ACCOUNT TITLES AND EXPLANATION	P.R.	DEBIT	CREDIT

DATE	ACCOUNT TITLES AND EXPLANATION	P.R.	DEBIT	CREDIT

Name _____

EXERCISE 9–2

Part 1

Part 2

	YEAR 1	YEAR 2	YEAR 3
Sales			
Cost of goods sold:			
Beginning inventory			
Purchases			
Goods avail. for sale			
Ending inventory			
Cost of goods sold			
Gross profit from sales			

EXERCISE 9–4

GENERAL JOURNAL   Page 1

DATE	ACCOUNT TITLES AND EXPLANATION	P.R.	DEBIT	CREDIT

| PRODUCT | UNITS ON HAND | PER UNIT | | TOTAL COST | TOTAL NET REALIZABLE VALUE | LOWER OF COST OR NRV |
		COST	NET REALIZABLE VALUE			

EXERCISE 9-6

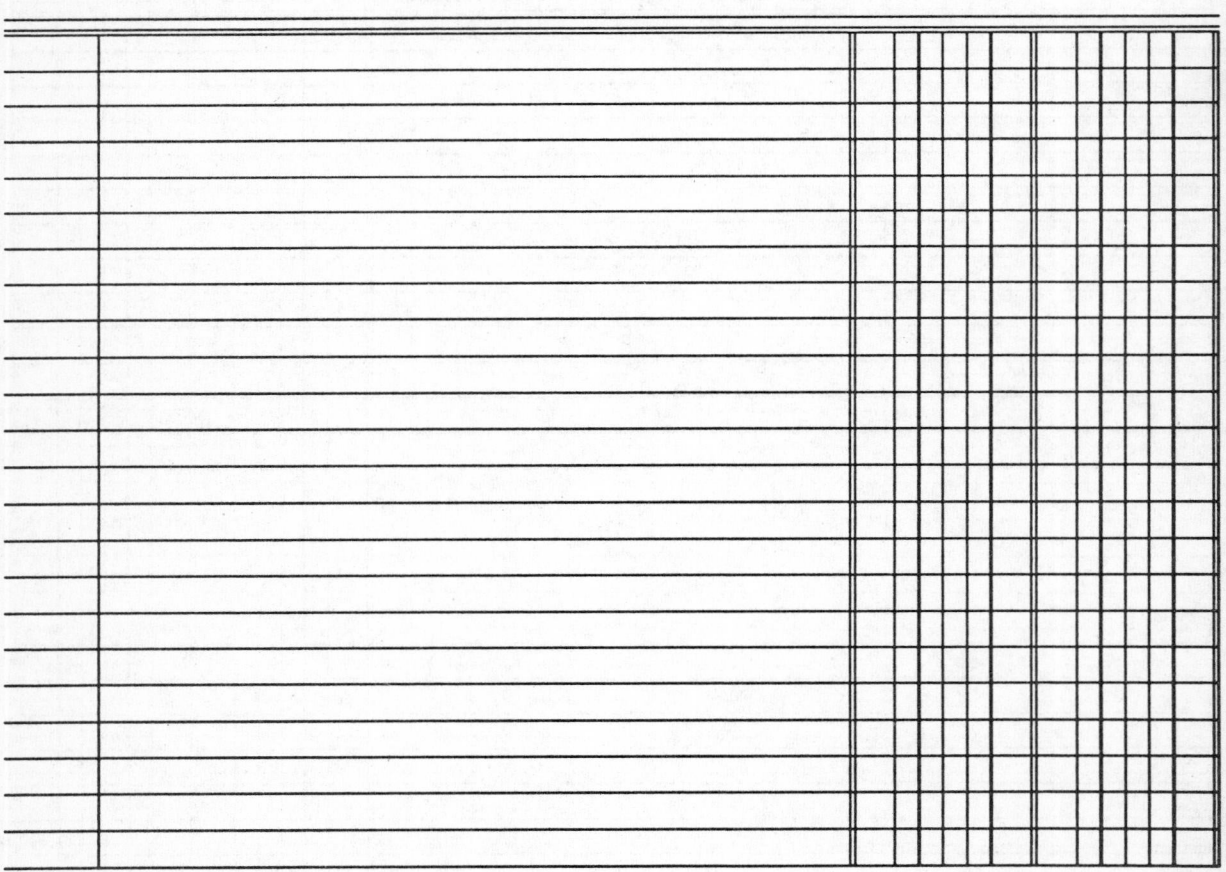

EXERCISE 9–8

Parts 1 and 2

WEIGHTED-AVERAGE COST

LIFO

FIFO

Name _____

	1994	1995	1996

Name _____

PRODUCT	UNITS ON HAND	PER UNIT		TOTAL COST	TOTAL NRV	LOWER OF COST OR NRV (by product)
		COST	REPLACEMENT COST			

Name _____

Part 1

_____
_____
_____
_____
_____
_____
_____
_____
_____
_____
_____
_____
_____
_____
_____
_____
_____
_____
_____
_____
_____

Part 2

_____
_____
_____
_____
_____
_____
_____
_____
_____
_____
_____
_____
_____
_____
_____
_____
_____
_____
_____
_____

Part 1

Part 2

Case 1

PRODUCT	UNITS ON HAND	PER UNIT		TOTAL COST	TOTAL MARKET	LOWER OF COST OR MARKET (by product)
		COST	MARKET			

Case 2

PRODUCT	UNITS ON HAND	PER UNIT		TOTAL COST	TOTAL MARKET	LOWER OF COST OR MARKET (by product)
		COST	MARKET			

	1996	1997	1998

Part 1

Item _____   Location in stockroom _____

Maximum _____   Minimum _____

DATE	PURCHASED			SOLD			BALANCE		
	UNITS	COST	TOTAL	UNITS	COST	TOTAL	UNITS	COST	TOTAL

Part 2

Item _____   Location in stockroom _____

Maximum _____   Minimum _____

DATE	PURCHASED			SOLD			BALANCE		
	UNITS	COST	TOTAL	UNITS	COST	TOTAL	UNITS	COST	TOTAL

Part 3

GENERAL JOURNAL   Page 1

DATE	ACCOUNT TITLES AND EXPLANATION	P.R.	DEBIT	CREDIT

EXERCISE 10–2

GENERAL JOURNAL   Page 1

DATE	ACCOUNT TITLES AND EXPLANATION	P.R.	DEBIT	CREDIT

GENERAL JOURNAL

DATE	ACCOUNT TITLES AND EXPLANATION	P.R.	DEBIT	CREDIT

GENERAL JOURNAL   Page 1

DATE	ACCOUNT TITLES AND EXPLANATION	P.R.	DEBIT	CREDIT

EXERCISE 10–5

GENERAL JOURNAL

Page 1

DATE	ACCOUNT TITLES AND EXPLANATION	P.R.	DEBIT	CREDIT

EXERCISE 10–7

Account	P.R.	Debit	Credit
Sales			00000
Less Sales Returns		0000	
Sales Discounts		0000	0000
Net Sales			0000
Cost of Goods Sold			
Merchandise Inv Dec 31 96		0000	
Purchases	0000		
Less Purchase Retur	000		
Purchase Dis	000	0000	
Net Purchases	0000		
Add transportation in	0000		
Cost Cost of Goods Purchase		0000	
Goods Avail for sale		0000	
Merch end Mont		000	
Cost Cost of Goods Soft			0000
Gross Profit from Sal			0000

Sales
    Less Sales Return + Allow
         Sales Discount
Net Sales

Cost of Goods Sold
    Merchandise Inv
    Purchases
         Less Purchase Returns + Allow
              Purchase Discounts
    Net Purchases
    Add: Transportation In
    Cost of Goods Purchased
    Goods Avail for Sale
    Merchandise Inv end OP
    Cost of Goods Sold
Gross Profit from Sales

Operating Expenses
    Selling Expenses
         Total

Merchand Inv
Sales
Purchase Returns
    Discounts
    Income summary

Income summary
    Merchandise Inv
    Sales Returns
    Sales Discounts

Income summary
    capital

Capital
    withdrawls

Nov 1   Petty cash   75
        cash   75

Misc expence

Nov 2 $10
Nov 3 $20
Nov 4 $20   N6 50

Transportation In
Nov 5   delivery   600
Nov 6   delivery   600   400

Deliv
Nov customer paid   500

Name _____

GENERAL JOURNAL

DATE	ACCOUNT TITLES AND EXPLANATION	P.R.	DEBIT	CREDIT

CHEQUE REGISTER

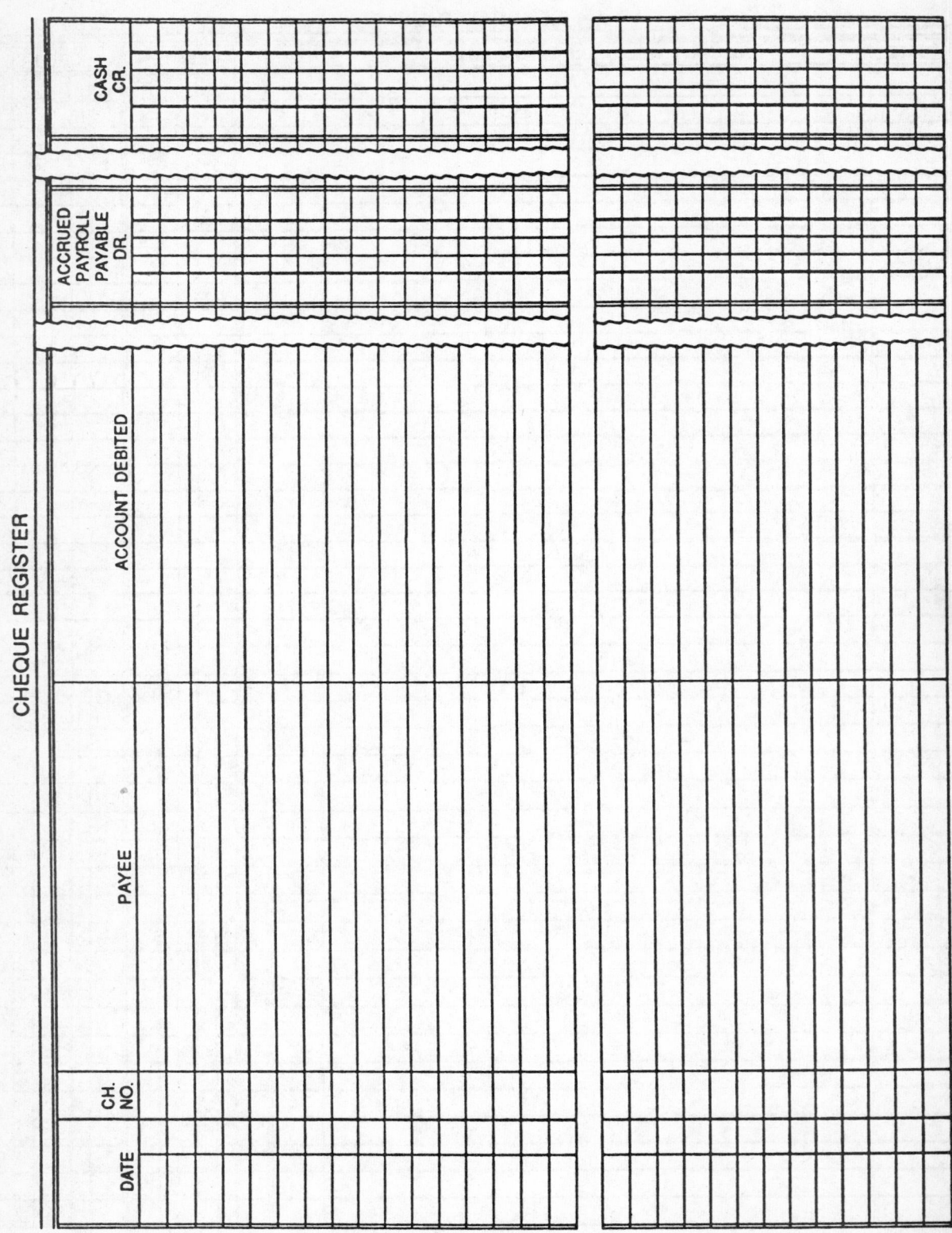

GENERAL JOURNAL

DATE	ACCOUNT TITLES AND EXPLANATION	P.R.	DEBIT	CREDIT

PAYROLL REGISTER

EMPLOYEE	CLOCK CARD NUMBER	DAILY TIME							TOTAL HOURS	O.T. HOURS	REG. PAY RATE	REGULAR PAY	O.T. PREMIUM PAY	GROSS PAY	
		M	T	W	T	F	S	S							
															1
															2
															3
															4
															5
															6
															7
															8
															9

CHEQUE REGISTER

DATE		CH. NO.	PAYEE	ACCOUNT DEBITED	
					1
					2
					3
					4
					5
					6
					7
					8

WEEK ENDED

	DEDUCTIONS						PAYMENT		DISTRIBUTION	
	UNEM-PLOYMENT INS.	CANADA PENSION PLAN	INCOME TAXES	HOSPITAL INSUR-ANCE	UNION DUES	TOTAL DEDUC-TIONS	NET PAY	CHEQUE NUMBER	OFFICE SALARIES EXPENSE	SERVICE WAGES EXPENSE
1										
2										
3										
4										
5										
6										
7										
8										
9										

	P.R.	OTHER ACCOUNTS DR.	ACCOUNTS PAYABLE DR.	SALARIES PAYABLE DR.	CASH CR.
1					
2					
3					
4					
5					
6					
7					
8					

GENERAL JOURNAL

DATE	ACCOUNT TITLES AND EXPLANATION	P.R.	DEBIT	CREDIT

DATE	ACCOUNT TITLES AND EXPLANATION	P.R.	DEBIT	CREDIT

PAYROLL REGISTER

| EMPLOYEE | CLOCK CARD NUMBER | DAILY TIME | | | | | | | TOTAL HOURS | O.T. HOURS | REG. PAY RATE | EARNINGS | | | |
		M	T	W	T	F	S	S				REGULAR PAY	O.T. PREMIUM PAY	GROSS PAY	
															1
															2
															3
															4
															5
															6
															7
															8
															9

CHEQUE REGISTER

DATE	CH. NO.	PAYEE	ACCOUNT DEBITED	
				1
				2
				3
				4
				5
				6
				7
				8

WEEK ENDED

	DEDUCTIONS						PAYMENT		DISTRIBUTION		
	UNEM-PLOY-MENT INS.	CANADA PENSION PLAN	INCOME TAXES	MEDICAL INSUR-ANCE	UNION DUES	TOTAL DEDUC-TIONS	NET PAY	CHEQUE NUMBER	SALES SALARIES	OFFICE SALARIES	SHOP SALARIES
1											
2											
3											
4											
5											
6											
7											
8											
9											

	P.R.	OTHER ACCOUNTS DR.	ACCOUNTS PAYABLE DR.	ACCRUED PAYROLL PAYABLE DR.	PURCHASES DISCOUNT CR.	CASH CR.
1						
2						
3						
4						
5						
6						
7						
8						

GENERAL JOURNAL

DATE	ACCOUNT TITLES AND EXPLANATION	P.R.	DEBIT	CREDIT

DATE	CH. NO.	PAYEE	ACCOUNT DEBITED	P.R.	OTHER ACCOUNTS DR.	ACCRUED PAYROLL PAYABLE DR.	CASH CR.

GENERAL JOURNAL

DATE	ACCOUNT TITLES AND EXPLANATION	P.R.	DEBIT	CREDIT

GENERAL JOURNAL

DATE	ACCOUNT TITLES AND EXPLANATION	P.R.	DEBIT	CREDIT

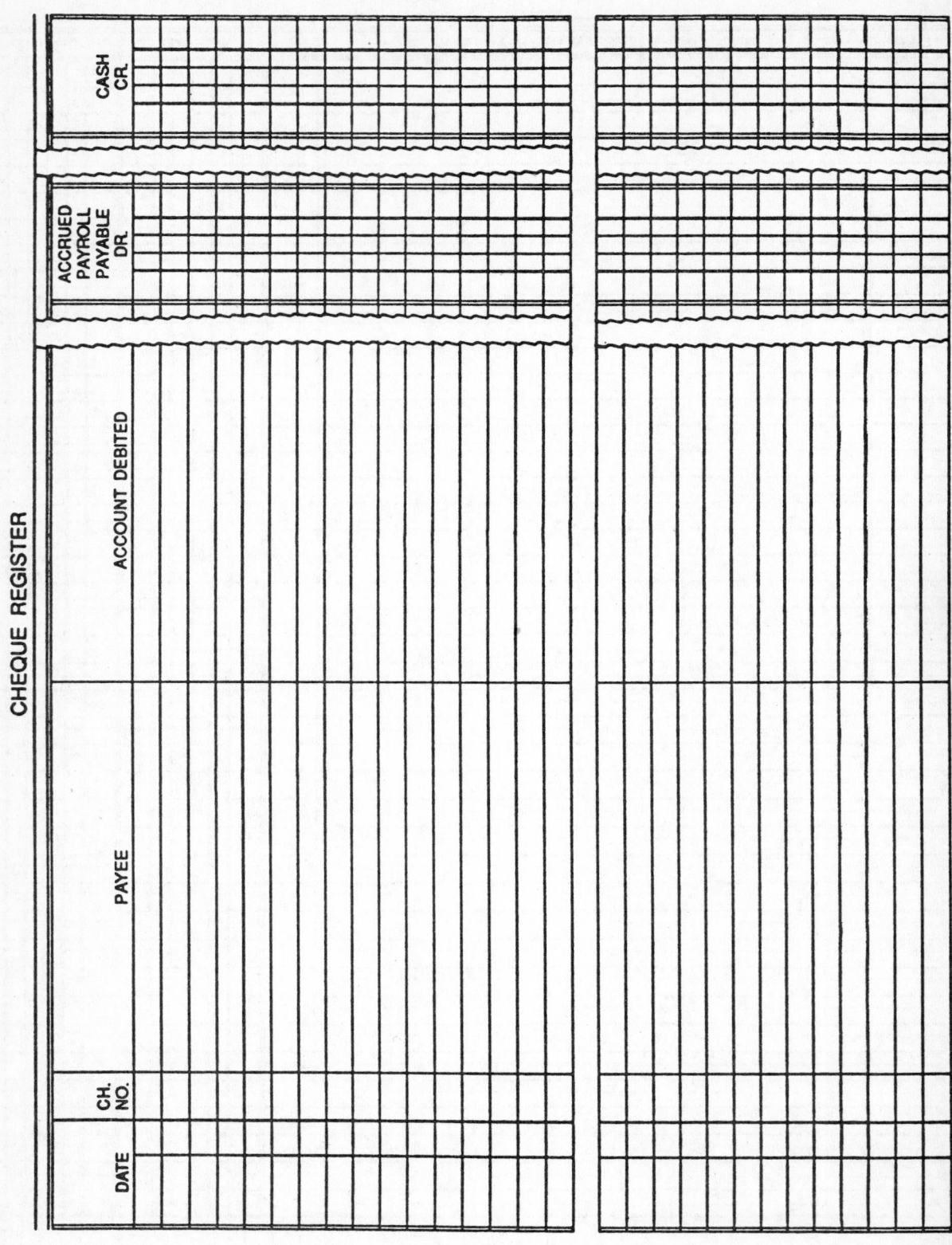

CHEQUE REGISTER

DATE	CH. NO.	PAYEE	ACCOUNT DEBITED	ACCRUED PAYROLL PAYABLE DR.	CASH CR.

Name _____

GENERAL JOURNAL

DATE	ACCOUNT TITLES AND EXPLANATION	P.R.	DEBIT	CREDIT

PAYROLL REGISTER

EMPLOYEE	CLOCK CARD NUMBER	DAILY TIME								TOTAL HOURS	O.T. HOURS	REG. PAY RATE	REGULAR PAY	O.T. PREMIUM PAY	GROSS PAY	
		M	T	W	T	F	S	S								
																1
																2
																3
																4
																5
																6
																7
																8
																9

CHEQUE REGISTER

DATE		CH. NO.	PAYEE	ACCOUNT DEBITED	
					1
					2
					3
					4
					5
					6
					7
					8

WEEK ENDED

	UNEM-PLOYMENT INS.		CANADA PENSION PLAN		INCOME TAXES		HOSPITAL INSUR-ANCE		UNION DUES		TOTAL DEDUC-TIONS		NET PAY		CHEQUE NUMBER	OFFICE SALARIES EXPENSE		PLANT SALARIES	
	DEDUCTIONS													PAYMENT			DISTRIBUTION			
1																				
2																				
3																				
4																				
5																				
6																				
7																				
8																				
9																				

	P.R.	OTHER ACCOUNTS DR.	ACCOUNTS PAYABLE DR.	SALARIES PAYABLE DR.	CASH CR.
1					
2					
3					
4					
5					
6					
7					
8					

GENERAL JOURNAL

DATE	ACCOUNT TITLES AND EXPLANATION	P.R.	DEBIT	CREDIT

DATE	ACCOUNT TITLES AND EXPLANATION	P.R.	DEBIT	CREDIT

PAYROLL REGISTER

| EMPLOYEE | CLOCK CARD NUMBER | DAILY TIME | | | | | | | TOTAL HOURS | O.T. HOURS | REG. PAY RATE | EARNINGS | | | |
		M	T	W	T	F	S	S				REGULAR PAY	O.T. PREMIUM PAY	GROSS PAY	
															1
															2
															3
															4
															5
															6
															7
															8
															9

CHEQUE REGISTER

DATE		CH. NO.	PAYEE	ACCOUNT DEBITED	
					1
					2
					3
					4
					5
					6
					7
					8

WEEK ENDED

	DEDUCTIONS						PAYMENT		DISTRIBUTION		
	UNEM-PLOY-MENT INS.	CANADA PENSION PLAN	INCOME TAXES	MEDICAL INSUR-ANCE	UNION DUES	TOTAL DEDUC-TIONS	NET PAY	CHEQUE NUMBER	SALES SALARIES	OFFICE SALARIES	SHOP SALARIES
1											
2											
3											
4											
5											
6											
7											
8											
9											

	P.R.	OTHER ACCOUNTS DR.	ACCOUNTS PAYABLE DR.	ACCRUED PAYROLL PAYABLE DR.	PURCHASES DISCOUNT CR.	CASH CR.
1						
2						
3						
4						
5						
6						
7						
8						

GENERAL JOURNAL

DATE	ACCOUNT TITLES AND EXPLANATION	P.R.	DEBIT	CREDIT

DATE	CH. NO.	PAYEE	ACCOUNT DEBITED	P.R.	OTHER ACCOUNTS DR.	ACCRUED PAYROLL PAYABLE DR.	CASH CR.

GENERAL JOURNAL

DATE	ACCOUNT TITLES AND EXPLANATION	P.R.	DEBIT	CREDIT

Notes

Notes

Notes

Notes

Notes

Notes

Notes

Notes

Notes

Notes